NEW 2018

COMMON CORE MATH
GRADE 7

PART II: FREE RESPONSE

Visit **www.argoprep.com** to get
FREE access to our online platform.

1000+ Minutes of Video Explanations and more!

Authors: Kellie Zimmer
Anayet Chowdhury
Eduard Suleyman
Vladislav Suleyman

Design: Vladislav Suleyman

At Argo Brothers, we are dedicated to providing quality and effective supplemental practice for your child. We would love to hear your honest feedback and **review** of our workbooks on **Amazon**.

Argo Brothers is one of the leading providers of supplemental educational products and services. We offer affordable and effective test prep solutions to educators, parents and students. Learning should be fun and easy! For that reason, most of our workbooks come with detailed video answer explanations taught by one of our fabulous instructors. Our goal is to make your life easier, so let us know how we can help you by e-mailing us at **info@argobrothers.com**.

 ARGO BROTHERS

OTHER BOOKS BY ARGO BROTHERS

Here are some other test prep workbooks by Argo Brothers you may be interested in. All of our workbooks come equipped with detailed video explanations to make your learning experience a breeze! Subscribe to our mailing list at www.argobrothers.com to receive custom updates about your education.

GRADE 2

GRADE 3

GRADE 4
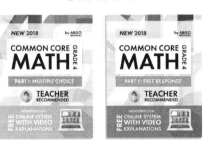

GRADE 5
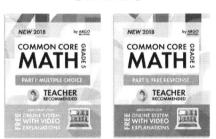

GRADE 6

GRADE 7

GRADE 4

GRADE 5

TABLE OF CONTENTS

HOW TO USE THE BOOK

This workbook is designed to give lots of practice with the math Common Core State Standards (CCSS). By practicing and mastering this entire workbook, your child will become very familiar and comfortable with the state math exam. If you are a teacher using this workbook for your student's, you will notice each question is labeled with the specific standard so you can easily assign your students problems in the workbook. This workbook takes the CCSS and divides them up among 20 weeks. By working on these problems on a daily basis, students will be able to (1) find any deficiencies in their understanding and/or practice of math and (2) have small successes each day that will build proficiency and confidence in their abilities.

You can find detailed video explanations to each problem in the book by visiting:
www.argoprep.com

We strongly recommend watching the videos as it will reinforce the fundamental concepts. Please note, scrap paper may be necessary while using this workbook so that the student has sufficient space to show their work.

Please note, scrap paper may be necessary while using this workbook so that the student has sufficient space to show their work.

For a detailed overview of the Common Core State Standards for 7th grade, please visit: www.corestandards.org/Math/Content/7/introduction/

For more practice with 7th Grade Math, be sure to check out our other book, Common Core Math Workbook Grade 7: Multiple Choice

WEEK 1

This week you will begin by using strategies to add and subtract rational numbers as well as find pairs of numbers that have a sum of zero.

You can find detailed video explanations to each problem in the book by visiting:
ArgoPrep.com

DAY 1

TIP of the **DAY**

---

1. Find the value of the expression below.

74.9 + 5.23 − 81.4 − 16

7.NS.1

---

2. Altitude above sea level is given in positive values. Below sea level is given in negative values. If a hiker started at sea level and increased his altitude by 75 meters before decreasing his altitude by 112 meters, what was his final altitude?

7.NS.1

---

3. Ansel owed $70 to his friend. He also owes another $24 to his sister. Write an equation that could be used to find how much money Ansel owes.

7.NS.1

---

4. Below are some transactions (in dollars) that Ana made to her bank account.

Deposit	Withdrawals
134.17	- 396.52
900	- 602.96

If Ana's account had $298 before any deposits or withdrawals, what was her final balance?

7.NS.1

---

5. This morning it was −11.5°F. If the temperature dropped 4.8°F in the afternoon, what was the temperature in the afternoon?

7.NS.1

1. Altitude above sea level is given in positive values and below sea level is given in negative values. If the rescue helicopter was hovering at 350 feet above sea level and the man being rescued was at 478 feet below sea level, what was the distance between the helicopter and the man being rescued?

7.NS.1

2. Below are some transactions (in dollars) that Alfred made to his bank account.

297.23	– 523.08	– 219.44	106.79

If Alfred's account had $576 before any deposits or withdrawals, what was his final balance?

7.NS.1

3. Alexis started with $106. She paid back $50 to her brother and her sister borrowed $12. Write an expression that could be used to find how much cash Alexis now has.

7.NS.1

4. The temperature was 58.7°F. If it rose 5.1°F, what is the new temperature?

7.NS.1

5. Altitude above sea level is given in positive values and below sea level is given in negative values. Aimee was hiking and the trail started at 92 yards below sea level. The first stop on the trail was up 63 yards. What is the altitude of the first stop?

7.NS.1

6. Find the value of the expression below.

75 + 39 − 84 − 61

7.NS.1

DAY 3

When adding one positive and one negative number, find the difference between the 2 numbers themselves (or magnitude) and keep the sign of the number that has the larger magnitude.

1. If the temperature Tuesday night was 27.1°C. and the temperature was 32.1°C the next morning. How much did the temperature change?

7.NS.1

2. Below are the transactions (in dollars) that Alex made to his bank account last week.

706.34	- 529.42	18.10	- 375.08

If Alex's account had $1,109.52 before any deposits or withdrawals, what was his account balance at the end of the week?

7.NS.1

3. If Benji started his trek at 315 feet below sea level and then decreased his altitude by 110 feet, what was his new altitude?

7.NS.1

4. Find the value of the expression below.

$212 - 75.8 + 63.29 - 140.6 = ?$

7.NS.1

5. In Petosky, Michigan it was −13.7°F. In Bay City Michigan the temperature was 10.9°F. How many degrees colder was it in Petosky?

7.NS.1

6. Thursday night it was −7.9°C. If the temperature dropped 4.2°C overnight, what was the temperature Friday morning?

7.NS.1

---

1. What is the decimal equivalent of $\frac{3}{8}$?

7.NS.2

---

2. What is the product of $\left(\frac{3}{5}\right) \times \left(-\frac{2}{8}\right)$?

7.NS.2

---

3. Convert $\frac{1}{6}$ to its decimal equivalent using long division.

7.NS.2

---

4. What is the decimal equivalent of $\frac{8}{9}$?

7.NS.2

---

5. What is the quotient of $\left(-\frac{2}{5}\right) \div \left(\frac{3}{5}\right)$?

7.NS.2

---

6. Arnold is subtracting 18 from 23. Write an expression that could be used to find the difference between 18 and 23.

7.NS.1

DAY 5 ASSESSMENT

---

1. Below are some transactions that Avery made to her bank account.

435.01	- 500
179.88	- 426.32

If Avery's account had $857.64 before any deposits or withdrawals, what was her final balance?

7.NS.1

---

2. Altitude above sea level is given in positive values and below sea level is given in negative values. If Acadia started at 768 feet below sea level and then increased her altitude by 512 feet, what is her altitude now?

7.NS.1

---

3. Arabella is subtracting 17 from 11. Write an equation that could be used to find the difference between 17 and 11.

7.NS.1

---

4. Convert $\frac{7}{11}$ to its decimal equivalent.

7.NS.2

---

5. What is the decimal equivalent of $\frac{2}{5}$?

7.NS.2

DAY 6 CHALLENGE QUESTION

Wednesday night it was −15°C. If the temperature rose 13.5°C overnight, what was the temperature Thursday morning?

7.NS.1

Week 2 will allow you to practice multiplying and dividing rational numbers, including fractions. You can also use different properties of operations to solve real-world problems that involve all 4 operations. You will also be able to check your conversions as you change fractions to decimals.

You can find detailed video explanations to each problem in the book by visiting: ArgoPrep.com

DAY 1

Often when the numerator is divided by the denominator in a fraction, the result will be a decimal number that will either terminate or repeat.

TIP of the DAY

---

1. Convert $\frac{369}{1000}$ to its decimal equivalent.

7.NS.2

---

2. What is the decimal equivalent of $\frac{24}{30}$?

7.NS.2

---

3. What is the product of $\left(-\frac{7}{12}\right) \times \left(-\frac{9}{8}\right)$?

7.NS.2

---

4. What is the decimal equivalent of $\frac{7}{8}$?

7.NS.2

---

5. What is the quotient of $\left(\frac{2}{7}\right) \div \left(\frac{-4}{3}\right)$?

7.NS.2

---

6. Below are the withdrawals and deposits that Andre' made to his bank account last month.

- 182.36	- 560.24	- 97.03	824.57

If Andre's account had $518.40 before any deposits or withdrawals, what was his account balance at the end of the month?

7.NS.1

In word problems, try to find the operation(s) to use. You know the only operations that can be used are addition, subtraction, multiplication and/or division.

DAY 2

---

1. What is the decimal equivalent of $\frac{13}{4}$?

7.NS.2

---

2. What is the product of $\left(-\frac{1}{4}\right) \times \left(-\frac{11}{8}\right)$?

7.NS.2

---

3. Find the value of the expression below.

$-198 + 41.75 + 62.3 - 50.7$

7.NS.1

---

4. There are 20 students in Mrs. Boyer's homeroom. Thirteen of those students are boys. Write the fraction of boys as a decimal number.

7.NS.2

---

5. Write a decimal number that is equal to $\frac{3}{5}$.

7.NS.2

---

6. The Downer Trail begins at − 87 yards altitude and then ends with an altitude of 256 yards. What is the change in altitude from the beginning of the trail to the end?

7.NS.1

DAY 3

1. Six days last month it rained 4.5 inches. It rained 5 inches on 7 days last month. How many inches did it rain on those 13 days?

7.NS.3

2. Boris ran 7.9 miles each weekday last week and 13.2 miles each day of the weekend. What was the total distance Boris ran last week?

7.NS.3

3. Beth makes $10.25/hour and Bartley makes $11.50 an hour. If Beth worked 23 hours and Bartley worked 17 hours, what was the difference in the amount of money they each earned?

7.NS.3

4. Cana bought 9 packages of chocolate chips and 12 packages of flour. If the flour cost $5.19 per package and the chocolate chips were $2.28 per package, what was the cost for all of the items?

7.NS.3

5. Three moms bought some candy to share for Halloween. Each pound of candy was $4.15 each. They bought 9 pounds of candy. If they also shared the price, how much money would each mom contribute?

7.NS.3

6. Monday night it was - 1.3°C. If the temperature dropped 1.3°C overnight, what was the temperature Tuesday morning?

7.NS.1

1. Amelia began her hike at 1,652 feet above sea level. She then hiked down 2,403 feet, decreased her altitude by another 489 feet and then increased her altitude by 278 feet. What is Amelia's final altitude?

7.NS.3

2. On his trip, Buddy drove 55 mph for 1 hour, 65 mph for 3 hours and 50 mph for 2 hours. What was the distance of Buddy's trip?

7.NS.3

3. Bobby did chores every single day in September. It took Bobby $\frac{3}{4}$ hours to complete his chores on 20 of the days. The remaining 10 days of the month it took him 1 hour to complete his chores. How many hours did Bobby do chores in September?

7.NS.3

4. Alyse owed $501.64 on her credit card. She made a payment of $418 and then charged another $672.36. What does Alyse still owe on her credit card?

7.NS.3

5. Bianca talked on the phone for 2.8 hours on 3 days during the week. The other days of the week she only talked 1.75 hours. How much time did Bianca talk on the phone last week?

7.NS.3

6. Amir was sowing soybeans. He planted 3,296 plants and then had to remove 407 plants. He sowed another 2 rows that each contained 518 plants. How many plants are in Amir's garden now?

7.NS.3

DAY 5 ASSESSMENT

1. At Camp Gilman it costs $459 for a Tadpole camper, $499 for a Tamarack camper and $520 for a Triathlon camper. If there are 26 Tadpole campers, 10 Tamarack campers and 4 Triathlons, what is the total cost for these camp registrations?

   7.NS.3

2. For a wedding, the bride had 215 bags of popcorn that cost $1.40 each. She served 198 people, with the cost being $20.75 per plate. The photographer and caterer cost $850 each and the hall was $3,614. What was the total cost for the bride's wedding reception?

   7.NS.3

3. A hummingbird flies forward 149 meters, backwards 57 meters and forward 23 meters, Write an equation that can be used to find how far forward the hummingbird flew.

   7.NS.3

4. Aggie slept for $\frac{3}{5}$ of an hour in the car, slept for 1.3 hours at naptime and fell asleep again in the afternoon for another 90 minutes. How much time was Aggie asleep?

   7.NS.3

5. In Lakeland, Florida it was 81.2°F but the temperature dropped 14.8°F. Now what is the temperature in Lakeland?

   7.NS.1

6. What is the product of $\left(-\frac{4}{5}\right) \times \left(\frac{7}{18}\right)$?

   7.NS.2

DAY 6
CHALLENGE
QUESTION

At the beginning of the month Abraham had $4,230 for his expenses. He budgeted $915 for his mortgage, $365 for groceries, $287 for utilities and $194 for entertainment. If he stuck to his budget, how much money would he have available at the end of the month?

7.NS.1

This week you will be able to add, subtract, factor and expand algebraic expressions using the properties of operations.

You can find detailed video explanations to each problem in the book by visiting: ArgoPrep.com

When factoring, you should be able to multiply the factors in your answer and get the original expression.

TIP of the DAY

---

1. Factor: $24ab - 12b$

7.EE.1

---

2. Which property is shown below?

$17c + 4c + 6c = 4c + 6c + 17c$

7.EE.1

---

3. Write a simplified expression that is equivalent to $(7x + 8) - (5 - 3x)$.

7.EE.1

---

4. Factor: $105d + 77de$

7.EE.1

---

5. What is the value of the expression below?

$708.1 - 526.49 - 18.37 - 142$

7.NS.1

---

6. Write an expression that is equivalent to $(h + 8) + (3h - 1)$

7.EE.1

TIP of the DAY *$3(m-5) = 3m - 15$ is an example of the Distributive Property.*

DAY 2

1. Which property is shown below?

$8u \times (6v \times 2w) = (6v \times 2w) \times 8u$

7.EE.1

2. Factor $36jk - 32k$

7.EE.1

3. Write an expression that is equivalent to $7 - e + 7e - 12$.

7.EE.1

Use the steps below to answer questions 4 – 5.

Step 1: $\frac{1}{4}(16a + 24b + 12a - 8b)$

Step 2: $4a + 6b + 3a - 2b$

Step 3: $4a + 3a + 6b - 2b$

Step 4: $7a + 4b$

4. Which property is used between Steps 1 and 2?

7.EE.1

5. Which property is used between Steps 2 and 3?

7.EE.1

6. Rewrite the following expression using the Associative Property:

$(4x + 9x) + 12x$

7.EE.1

DAY 3

When there is a negative sign to the left of a set of parentheses, every term within the parentheses is subtracted.

TIP of the DAY

Use the steps below to answer questions 1 – 2.

Step 1: $\frac{3}{4}$ (12p + 20q)

Step 2: 9p + 15q

Step 3: 3 (3p + 5q)

Step 4: 3 (5q + 3p)

---

1. Which property is used between Steps 1 and 2?

7.EE.1

---

2. Which property is used between Steps 3 and 4?

7.EE.1

---

3. Write an expression that is equivalent to $12c - 4c - 7 + 12c - 2$.

7.EE.1

---

4. Factor: $125st + 50str$

7.EE.1

---

5. Yesterday it was −6.2°C. Overnight the temperature dropped 1.8°C. What was the temperature this morning?

7.NS.1

4u + 5v + w = w + 4u + 5v is is an example of the Commutative Property.

DAY 4

---

1. Write the best factorization for $64xyz - 32xy + 16xz$.

7.EE.1

---

2. Which property is shown in the expression below?

$4ab (5c - 7) = 20abc - 28ab$

7.EE.1

---

3. What is the product of $\left(\frac{20}{21}\right) \times \left(-\frac{14}{18}\right)$?

7.NS.2

---

4. Write a simplified expression that is equivalent to $2.5m - 19.8n + 7.8m + 11.3n$.

7.EE.1

---

5. Use the Distributive Property to expand $2s (3q - 5qr + 4pq)$

7.EE.1

---

6. What is the decimal equivalent of $\frac{1}{4}$?

7.NS.2

1. Write an expression that is equivalent to $7.2p + 3.8q - (4.8q - 5.1p)$.

7.EE.1

2. Use the Distributive Property to expand $5ab (6c + 5d - 10e)$.

7.EE.1

Use the steps below to answer questions 3 – 4.

Step 1: $(300ab + 450ac) + (250ad + 200ab)$

Step 2: $300ab + (450ac + 250ad) + 200ab$

Step 3: $500ab + 450ac + 250ad$

Step 4: $50a (10b + 9c + 5d)$

3. Which property is used between Steps 1 and 2?

7.EE.1

4. Which property is used between Steps 3 and 4?

7.EE.1

5. Write an expression that is equivalent to $\frac{3}{5} (u + 5v - 7w)$.

7.EE.1

DAY 6
CHALLENGE
QUESTION

What is the factorization of $56a - 14ab + 21ac$? 7.EE.1

Now that you know how to factor and expand expressions, in Week 4 you will be able to rewrite expressions in different forms so you can better understand a problem as well as its context.

You can find detailed video explanations to each problem in the book by visiting: ArgoPrep.com

DAY 1

TIP of the DAY

---

1. The cost of camp, c, is going to increase by 8% next summer. Write an expression that represents the expected cost for next summer's camp.

7.EE.2

Use the diagram below to answer questions 2 – 3. The rectangle shown is measured in centimeters and the width is represented by a. The other dimension is the length.

5a

a

---

2. Write a statement comparing the rectangle's length to its width.

7.EE.2

---

3. Write a statement comparing the rectangle's perimeter to its width.

7.EE.2

---

4. Bree bought a dress that was discounted 13%. If the non-sale price was d, write an expression that represents the cost Bree paid for the dress.

7.EE.2

---

5. What is the decimal equivalent of $\frac{8}{4}$?

7.NS.2

---

6. The number of employees is expected to increase by 9.5% next quarter. If e represents the current number of employees, write an expression that represents the expected number of employees.

7.EE.2

An increase or markup means more than 100% of the original number.

DAY 2

---

1. A shirt originally was priced at *s*. McClain bought it at a 20% discount. Write an expression that represents the cost McClain paid for the shirt.

7.EE.2

Use the diagram below to answer questions 2 – 3. The rectangle shown is measured in meters and the width is represented by *w*.

$\frac{1}{4}$ *w*

---

2. Write a statement comparing the rectangle's length (height) to its width.

7.EE.2

---

3. Write a statement comparing the rectangle's perimeter to its width.

7.EE.2

---

4. Write an expression that is equivalent to $(13x - 8y) - (8y - 2x)$.

7.EE.1

---

5. The store bought golf clubs that cost *g* dollars. The store marked up the clubs so they were 43% higher than what they bought them for. Write an expression to show the new cost of the golf clubs.

7.EE.2

---

6. What is the quotient of $\left(\frac{2}{3}\right) \div \left(\frac{15}{16}\right)$?

7.NS.2

---

1. The original cost of the tiara was t and it was not on sale. However, there was an $6\frac{1}{2}$% sales tax. What is the cost of the tiara, including tax?

7.EE.2

$\frac{1}{4}h$

h

Use the diagram below to answer questions 2 – 3. The rectangle shown is measured in yards and the height is represented by h. The other dimension is the width.

---

2. Write a statement comparing the rectangle's height to its width.

7.EE.2

---

3. Write a statement comparing the rectangle's perimeter to its width.

7.EE.2

---

4. Write an expression that is equivalent to $7a - 8b - 7a + 10b - 8b$.

7.EE.1

---

5. The original price of the belt was b. If Bastion had a coupon for 25% off, what was the sale price of the belt?

7.EE.2

---

6. Byron makes $13.25 an hour and Carlisle makes $10.17 an hour. If Byron worked 19 hours and Carlisle worked 27 hours, how much money did they earn altogether?

7.NS.3

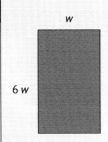
TIP of the **DAY**

---

w

Use the diagram below to answer questions 1 – 2. The rectangle shown is measured in centimeters and the width is represented by *w*. The other dimension is the length

6 *w*

---

1. Write a statement comparing the rectangle's length to its width.

7.EE.2

---

2. Write a statement comparing the rectangle's perimeter to its width.

7.EE.2

---

3. The music store bought a violin that cost *v* dollars. The store marked up the violin so it was 52% higher than what they bought it for. Write an expression to show the new cost of the violin.

7.EE.2

---

4. The population of Woodhaven, *W*, is expected to decrease by 4% over the next 10 years. Which expression shows the expected population of Woodhaven in 10 years?

7.EE.2

---

5. Chasity has a discount card that gives her 7% off the purchase of each pie. If *p* is the cost of a regular pie, how much does Chasity pay for her pie?

7.EE.2

---

6. Which property is being used in the expression below?

$(12w + 6w) + 8w = 12w + (6w + 8w)$

7.EE.1

1. Chuck must pay a sales tax of $11\frac{3}{4}$ % on each item he buys. If he buys a car that cost c, write an expression that represents the total cost Chuck must pay.

7.EE.2

2. Factor: $14ax + 35ay - 28az$.

7.EE.1

3. If the number of honey badgers, b, is expected to decrease by $4\frac{4}{5}$ % , write an expression that represents the number of honey badgers after the decrease.

7.EE.2

$\frac{1}{3}h$

h

Use the diagram below to answer questions 4 – 5. The rectangle shown is measured in inches where h is the height (or length). The other dimension is the width.

4. Write a statement comparing the rectangle's perimeter to its width.

7.EE.2

5. Write a statement comparing the rectangle's width to its height

7.EE.2

6. The current tuition, t, at South College is expected to rise $13\frac{1}{2}$ % over the next few years. What will the tuition be after that increase?

7.EE.2

DAY 6
CHALLENGE
QUESTION

Betsie bought a purse that was discounted 25%. Use p to equal the regular price of the purse and write an expression that shows how much Betsie paid for her purse.

7.EE.2

WEEK 5

ARGOPREP.COM

VIDEO EXPLANATIONS

Week 5 lets you find answers to real-world problems that require many steps.
You will use positive and negative rational numbers to solve these problems and also to check your answers to see if they make sense.

You can find detailed video explanations to each problem in the book by visiting: ArgoPrep.com

 # DAY 1

When adding or subtracting decimal numbers, you must first line up the decimal points vertically.

TIP of the **DAY**

---

1. Donna earned \$12.25 per hour. She got a new job in which she made 9% more. How much did she make per hour at her new job?

7.EE.3

---

2. The temperatures were recorded for 6 days. When the 6 temperatures are added together, the sum is −7.2°C. If 5 of the days' temperatures are −7.2°C, −8.5°C, 3.2°C, 4.1°C and −3.8°C, what was the temperature on the 6th day?

7.EE.3

---

3. A pair of sandals that regularly sell for \$45 was on sale for 35% off the regular price. What is the sale price?

7.EE.3

---

4. The table had $2\frac{1}{4}$ inches of file folders. If each folder is $\frac{1}{8}$ of an inch, how tall would the pile of folders be if 18 folders were added to the pile?

7.EE.3

---

5. Write an expression that is equivalent to: $12f - f + 8g - 9g - 3f$.

7.EE.1

---

6. The batting cage costs \$3.25 for every 15 pitches. Each batter gets 10 pitches. If there were 8 batters in the morning, 12 in the afternoon and 7 in the evening, how much money should have been deposited into the batting cage?

7.EE.3

TIP of the **DAY**

Terminating and repeating decimals are not equal. For example, 1/3 = 0.333..., which is NOT the same as 0.3.

DAY 2

---

1. Donovan recorded his scores each time he went golfing. His scores were − 7, 2, 3, 0, 4, 1 and − 3. What was his average score?

7.EE.3

---

2. Edward earns $9.35 per hour. Below you can see how many hours he worked last week. How much did Edward earn last week?

Wednesday	$5\frac{7}{8}$
Thursday	$7\frac{3}{4}$
Friday	$8\frac{3}{8}$
Saturday	$9\frac{1}{4}$

7.EE.3

---

3. Red Snapper is normally $4.39/lb. but you can purchase 19 pounds for $79.23, how much would you save per pound if you bought the larger package?

7.EE.3

---

4. Eve's bicycle tire had a leak. It originally held 14.5 pounds of pressure but was losing 0.7 pounds of pressure each hour. How many pounds of pressure would remain after 5 hours?

7.EE.3

---

5. Which property is shown in the equation below?

$(12k + k) + 6k = 6k + (12k + k)$

7.EE.1

When two positive numbers are added, the answer is also positive.

TIP of the DAY

If answers require rounding, round to the nearest cent or nearest hundredth.

---

1. Ebony earns $19.25 for the first 9 dresses she makes and $17.75 for every dress after that. If Ebony made $20\frac{1}{4}$ dresses, how much would she earn?

7.EE.3

---

2. Ethan recorded the balance on his lunch account for 5 days during the month. The balances were: −$13.50, $10.22, −$4.31, −$0.78, $3.67. What was the average of Ethan's lunch balance?

7.EE.3

---

3. Davida recorded the number of pounds her 10 puppies grew over a month. Their change in weights is shown below. What is the average weight change for the puppies?

$4\frac{3}{4}$ $3\frac{7}{8}$ $6\frac{7}{8}$ $5\frac{1}{2}$ $4\frac{1}{4}$ $4\frac{3}{4}$ $4\frac{3}{8}$ $5\frac{1}{4}$ $6\frac{1}{4}$ $5\frac{3}{8}$

7.EE.3

---

4. Dylan made $24.98 per hour until he was was injured. Then he took another job for 9% less. What is his new hourly rate?

7.EE.3

---

5. Dena kept track of the change in humidity for several weeks. Her results are shown here. If the humidity changes had a sum of −22.4%, what is the missing humidity change?

Number of Days	Change in Humidity
9	−2.1%
6	3.7%
7	−2.9%
4	−3.4%
2	?

7.NS.3

1. Felix was playing on the playground. The students had a large hopscotch-like board painted on the ground. Felix started on space #12. The teacher told him to move back 7 spaces, forward 18 spaces, back 3 spaces and then back another 12. Which space is Felix on now?

7.EE.3

2. Evalyn kept track of how much her 2 rose bushes grew every week. One grew $2\frac{3}{4}$, $2\frac{7}{8}$ and $3\frac{1}{8}$ inches and the second one grew $3\frac{1}{4}$, $2\frac{5}{8}$ and $2\frac{1}{8}$ inches. How much more did one rose bush grow than the other?

7.EE.3

3. The oil tanker can hold 3,500 gallons of oil. If it could take on $12\frac{1}{2}$ gallons every hour, how long would it take the tanker to fill?

7.EE.3

4. Dawnelle needs material for coats she is making. The chart below shows how many coats she is making and how many yards of material she needs for one coat. How much material does Dawnelle need in total?

Pattern	Number of Coats	Material Needed / Coat
A	6	$6\frac{3}{4}$ yards
B	2	$8\frac{2}{3}$ yards
C	5	$7\frac{1}{3}$ yards

7.EE.3

5. What is the quotient of $\left(-\frac{15}{21}\right) \div \left(\frac{14}{10}\right)$?

7.NS.2

1. Frederick earns \$21.08 per hour. Last week he worked $32\frac{3}{4}$ hours. How much did Frederick earn last week?

7.EE.3

2. A table typically costs \$859. It was on sale for 31% off the regular price. What was the sale price?

7.EE.3

3. What is the sum of $31\frac{2}{3} - 20\frac{3}{4} - 18\frac{2}{3} + 13\frac{7}{8}$?

7.EE.3

4. Each ticket to Hockey Town is \$15.85 per visit. If you purchase the season pass, you can visit Hockey Town 12 times for \$150. If you purchased the season pass, how much would you save *per visit*?

7.EE.3

5. What is the average of the numbers below?

$21\frac{2}{3}$, $7\frac{1}{2}$, $-10\frac{3}{4}$, -12 , $9\frac{1}{3}$

7.EE.3

6. What is the decimal equivalent of $\frac{11}{8}$?

7.NS.2

DAY 6
CHALLENGE
QUESTION

The Native American squaw can braid $4\frac{5}{8}$ meters of rope each hour. If she has $3\frac{1}{4}$ meters already, how long will her rope be after 4 hours?

7.NS.2

By now you're familiar with solving real-world problems. This week you will be able to write your own equations and/or inequalities to solve these problems. You will also begin to solve linear equations by determining what steps to take first.

**You can find detailed video explanations to each problem in the book by visiting:
ArgoPrep.com**

---

1. Flora has 33 flowers and she can pick 7 flowers a minute. Write an equation that shows how many flowers, F, that Flora will have after M minutes.

7.EE.4

---

2. Ethan wants to purchase a car that costs $5,097. He can save $216 each month and he already has $3,186 saved. What is the minimum number of months it will take Ethan to be able to save enough money for the car?

7.EE.4

---

3. The taxi is $5.50 for any ride plus $1.35 per block. How many complete blocks can a passenger travel if they only have $35?

7.EE.4

---

4. Write an equation that could be used to find the perimeter of the figure shown below.

7.EE.4

---

5. Solve: $-4t < -16$

7.EE.4

---

6. The equation $m + 0.08m = 1.08m$ shows how much Blair paid for a meal, m, plus the tax for the meal. What was the tax rate?

7.EE.2

TIP of the **DAY**

Sometimes to solve an equation, a formula is necessary. Be sure to choose the correct formula.

DAY 2

---

1. Write an addition equation that could be used to find the perimeter of the figure shown below.

7.EE.4

---

2. If the area of a square is 169 m², write an multiplication equation to find P, the perimeter of the square.

7.EE.4

---

3. Solve: $5d \geq -60$

7.EE.4

---

4. Esther earns \$15/hour but has to pay a daily internet fee of \$8 for each day she works. Write an equation to show how much money, m, Esther has after working h hours on 3 days.

7.EE.4

---

5. What is the product of $\left(-\frac{4}{14}\right) \times \left(-\frac{8}{5}\right)$?

7.NS.2

---

6. Write an expression that is equivalent to $(23.6 - 7.1a - 4.2b) - (5.8b - 9a)$

7.EE.1

When solving equations, first try to isolate the variable term by itself on one side of the equal sign.

 TIP of the DAY

---

1. It is $79 to rent the car plus $25 per day. How many complete days can Gwen use the car if she doesn't want to spend more than $250?

7.EE.4

---

2. You are to solve the equation: $8y - 6 = 14$. What step should you take first?

7.EE.4

---

3. If the perimeter of a square is 360 inches, what is the length of the square?

7.EE.4

---

4. Figaro wants to purchase a go-kart for $835. Each week he earns $103 chopping wood. If he already has $208, how many weeks will it take Figaro until he can buy the go-kart?

7.EE.4

---

5. The non-sale price of the recliner was r. If Cammie had a coupon for 12.5% off, what was the sale price of the recliner?

7.EE.2

---

6. Forrest borrowed $D to purchase a motorcycle. Forrest has $231 and can earn $562 per week. Write an equation that shows D, the amount of the loan and w, the number of weeks that Forrest will need to work to be able to pay back his loan.

7.EE.4

TIP of the **DAY**

When solving equations, remember to perform the operations on both sides of the equation. If you subtract 2 from one side of the equation, you need to subtract 2 from the other side of the equation also.

DAY 4

1. Gilda wants to buy a car for $22,000. She has saved $11,000 so far and can commit $539 each month toward the purchase of the car. How many months will it take Gilda to save enough money to buy the car?

7.EE.4

2. If the perimeter of a rectangle is 210 inches and its length is 57 inches, write an equation that can be used to find the rectangle's width, *w*.

7.EE.4

3. You are to solve the equation: $12 = 3x - 5$. What should be your first step?

7.EE.4

4. George earns $15.80 per hour. Below you can see how many hours he worked last week. How much did George earn last week?

Monday	$11\frac{1}{8}$
Wednesday	12.4
Friday	$9\frac{3}{4}$

7.EE.3

5. Dionne earned $567 working 42 hours last week. If she gets a 10% raise, what will her new hourly rate be?

7.EE.3

1. Write an equation that could be used to find the perimeter of the figure below.

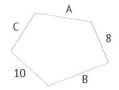

7.EE.4

2. You are to solve the inequality: $5a + 7 > -12$. What step should you take first?

7.EE.4

3. The area of a rectangle is 72 mm² and the length is 8 mm. What is the perimeter of the rectangle?

7.EE.4

4. Gus earned $318.75 last week and his schedule is below. How much does Gus earn per hour?

Wednesday	$3\frac{1}{4}$
Thursday	$7\frac{1}{3}$
Friday	$9\frac{1}{6}$
Sunday	$5\frac{3}{4}$

7.EE.3

5. Galina made d diamond rings last month. This month she made $8\frac{1}{2}$ % more than last month. What is the number of rings Galina made this month?

7.EE.2

DAY 6
CHALLENGE QUESTION

Gaston gets $12.57 for each pound of fish he sells. He also has to pay $1.08 to prepare each pound of fish. If f is the pounds of fish he sells, write an equation that shows P, Gaston's amount of profit.

7.EE.4

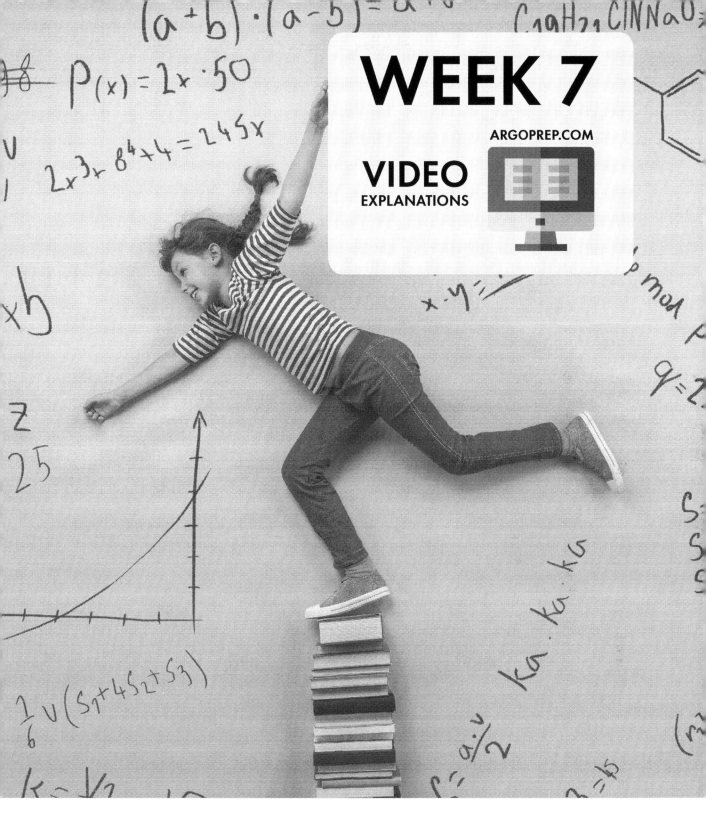

Week 7 provides practice using and finding unit rates and ratios. You will be able to find the constant of proportionality using graphs, tables and other visual representations.

You can find detailed video explanations to each problem in the book by visiting:
ArgoPrep.com

1. If 6 pomegranates weighed 9 pounds, how many pounds would you expect 1 pomegranate to weigh?

7.RP.1

2. Geoffrey was able to make $\frac{1}{2}$ of an omelet in 4 minutes. How many omelets could he make in 4 hours?

7.RP.1

3. Hattie could run 22 miles in 5 hours. How many miles could she run in 6 hours?

7.RP.1

4. Heather biked $8\frac{1}{4}$ km in 2 hours. How far could Heather bike in 7 hours?

7.RP.1

5. A truckload of concrete can be used for $42\frac{7}{8}$ yds² of roadway. A truckload weighs $12\frac{1}{4}$ tons. How many square yards could 1 ton of concrete cover?

7.RP.1

6. To solve the equation $\frac{2}{3}u = -8$, what step should you take first?

7.EE.4

1. Three cars can be made with $4\frac{1}{2}$ tons of metal. How many cars can be made with $19\frac{1}{2}$ tons of metal?

7.RP.1

2. Halle was able to knit $2\frac{1}{3}$ rows for the sweater in 12 minutes. How many rows could Halle knit in 2 hours?

7.RP.1

3. If 6 bags of pears weigh $12\frac{6}{7}$ pounds, how many pounds would you expect 1 bag of pears to weigh?

7.RP.1

4. Hershel was able to build 12 dressers in 10 hours. How many dressers could Hershel build in $5\frac{1}{2}$ hours?

7.RP.1

5. Heston was able to walk $\frac{1}{3}$ of a mile in 5 minutes. How far could Heston walk in 2 hours?

7.RP.1

6. Each hour Ira is able to mow 3 lawns. If he has already mowed 4 lawns, how many lawns will he have mowed after 5 more hours?

7.EE.4

 **DAY 3**

Variables represent real numbers so be sure to understand what the variable represents.

 **TIP** of the **DAY**

---

1. Iris used $\frac{9}{11}$ of a gallon of paint that covered $\frac{3}{4}$ of her room. How many gallons would it take to paint the entire room?

7.RP.1

---

2. What is the constant of proportionality for the table below?

x	y
1	2
4.5	9
3	6

7.RP.2

Use the tables below to answer questions 3 – 5.

Table A

x	y
2	3
8	12
4	6

Table B

x	y
5	7
7	9
9	11

Table C

x	y
2	6
3	9
1	3

---

3. Which table has a constant of proportionality of $\frac{3}{2}$?

7.RP.2

---

4. Which table shows a constant of proportionality of 3?

7.RP.2

---

5. Which table has NO constant of proportionality?

7.RP.2

1. Taffy was $8.97 per box. Write an equation that can be used to find C, the total cost for t boxes of taffy.

7.RP.2

2. What is the constant of proportionality for the figure below?

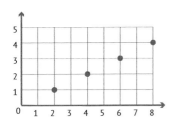

7.RP.2

Please use the tables below to answer questions 3 – 5.

Table A	
x	**y**
1	1
5	5
4	4

Table B	
x	**y**
5	2
10	4
15	6

Table C	
x	**y**
1	2
3	4
5	6

Table D	
x	**y**
1.5	6
0.5	2
2.3	9.2

3. Which table shows a constant of proportionality of 4?

7.RP.2

4. What is the constant of proportionality for Table A?

7.RP.2

5. Which table does NOT have a constant of proportionality?

7.RP.2

DAY 5 ASSESSMENT

1. What is the constant of proportionality for the table?

x	y
12	2.4
15	3
8	1.6

7.RP.2

2. Fuji apples cost $2.84 per pound. Write an equation that can be used to find C, the total cost for a pounds of apples.

7.RP.2

3. What is the constant of proportionality for the figure?

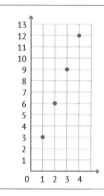

7.RP.2

4. A bag of compost weighing $5\frac{1}{3}$ pounds can be used on 8 m² of garden. How many square meters could 4 pounds of compost cover?

7.RP.1

5. Eisley is researching rental costs of different homes. Use the chart to find the 2 houses that have the same per night cost.

House	Nights	Cost
A	2	$125
B	4	$375
C	2	$250
D	5	$625

7.RP.2

DAY 6

CHALLENGE QUESTION

The constant of proportionality is $\frac{1}{4}$. If $x = 8$, what is the value of y?

7.RP.2

Week 8 gives lots of examples of percents and proportions as you find simple interest, taxes, discounts, markups and commissions. These topics are very relevant for people who shop, borrow money and/or work in sales.

You can find detailed video explanations to each problem in the book by visiting:
ArgoPrep.com

DAY 1

It is always important to ask yourself: "Percent of what?" Ten percent of 12 is different than 10% of 17.

1. There were 3,240 books in the school library. Twenty percent of the books were checked out on Friday. On Monday 25% of the remaining books were checked out. How many books were still at the library on Monday evening?

7.RP.3

2. The Cincinnati zoo had 25 snakes last year. This year they have 30 snakes. What is the percent increase in snakes from last year to this year?

7.RP.3

3. Irene purchased some earrings that regularly cost $55 for a friend's birthday. Irene used a "20% OFF" coupon. Irene's friend did not like the gift so she tried to return the earrings. She did not have the receipt so the store would only give her store credit for 50% of the purchase price. How much credit did Irene's friend receive?

7.RP.3

4. Janine got a car loan for $2,600. She was to pay that amount back along with an additional 6% interest. If she pays it off sooner, the loan company will take 1% off her total debt. If Janine pays early, how much money would Janine need to pay back on her loan?

7.RP.3

5. The temperature in Anchorage was 45°F on Wednesday. It increased by 20% on Thursday and then decreased by 10% on Friday. What was Friday's temperature?

7.RP.3

6. The number of peanuts harvested is expected to increase by 7.3% next summer. If p represents the current number of peanuts, write an expression that could be used to represent the expected number of peanuts.

7.EE.2

1. Last year the Pelicans won 80 games but only 32 games this year. What is the percent decrease in the number of games the Pelicans won last year to this year?

7.RP.3

2. Ella's score on Test 1 was 76. Her score on Test 2 was 98.8. What is the percent increase from Test 1 to Test 2?

7.RP.3

3. Davis started his job making $15 per hour. After 6 weeks he got a 5% raise. When he retired he was making 12% more than he had after the raise. What was Davis' hourly rate when he retired?

7.RP.3

4. The enrollment for Mr. Espinoza's class was 150 students. The next semester, he only had 96 students enroll. What was the percent decrease for the enrollment from last semester to this semester?

7.RP.3

5. Clucker laid 24 eggs last month. This month she only laid 21 eggs. What is the percent of decrease of eggs last month to eggs this month?

7.RP.3

6. What is the quotient of $\left(-\frac{3}{11}\right) \div \left(\frac{2}{12}\right)$?

7.NS.2

 **DAY 3**

 **TIP** of the **DAY**

---

1. If you pay this week, the drawing class costs $175. If you wait until next week, the cost increases by 15%. What will the cost be next week?

7.EE.3

---

2. On Quiz 1, Eleanor scored a 70. Quiz 2 she scored 20% better than Quiz 1. For Quiz 3 she scored 10% lower than Quiz 2. What was Eleanor's Quiz 3 score?

7.RP.3

The chart below shows the number of people who went to Fun World on different days during the week. **Use the table below to answer questions 3 – 4.**

Thursday	Friday	Saturday	Sunday
700	900	1,400	1,200

---

3. What is the percent decrease of people who went to Fun World on Sunday compared with those who went on Friday?

7.RP.3

---

4. What is the percent increase of people who went to Fun World on Thursday compared with those who went on Saturday?

7.RP.3

---

5. Find the value of the expression below.

29.4 − 1.402 + 13.56 − 18

7.NS.1

---

1. A desk normally sells for $565. It was on sale for 10% off the regular price during a store special. After the store special, the desk was increased by 10% more than the sales price. What is the new price?

7.RP.3

---

2. There are 3 sides to a triangle. One side is 100 inches long. The second side is 8% longer than the first side. The third side is 2% shorter than the second side. How long is the third side?

7.RP.3

---

3. Joanna's first nursing exam score was a 48. After she retook the exam her score was a 72. What is the percent increase from the first exam to the second exam?

7.RP.3

---

4. A deposit for a trip is $986. If you pay today, you can receive a 10% discount. What will the deposit be if you pay today?

7.EE.3

---

5. The price of a couch was $1899 but it was a floor model so the store discounted it 22%. There were 2 people interested in it so one agreed to pay 3% more than the asking price. How much money did the couch sell for?

7.RP.3

---

6. What is the decimal equivalent of $\frac{45}{6}$?

7.NS.2

DAY 5 ASSESSMENT

The chart below shows the number of candies that Mr. Larsen's class ate on different days during the week. **Use the table below to answer questions 1 – 3.**

Monday	Wednesday	Thursday	Friday
100	20	75	150

1. What is the percent decrease in candies on Friday compared to the number of candies on Thursday?

7.RP.3

2. What is the percent increase of candies on Wednesday compared to the number of candies on Monday?

7.RP.3

3. What is the percent decrease of candies on Monday compared to the number of candies on Wednesday?

7.RP.3

4. There are 4 sides to a quadrilateral. The first side is 28 mm. The second side is 25% longer than the first side. The third and fourth sides are 10% shorter than the second side. How long is the third side?

7.RP.3

5. Jared earns $9.89 an hour washing cars and Jalisa makes $10.17 an hour washing hair at the salon. If Jared worked 40 hours and Jalisa worked 33 hours, how much more money did Jared make?

7.NS.3

6. Which property is shown below?

$5u (3v - w) = 15uv - 5uw$

7.EE.1

DAY 6
CHALLENGE QUESTION

In his first race, Aiden's time was 120 seconds. His second race time was 108 seconds. Charity's first race time was 150 seconds and her second race time was 120 seconds. Which runner had the largest percent of decrease?

7.RP.3

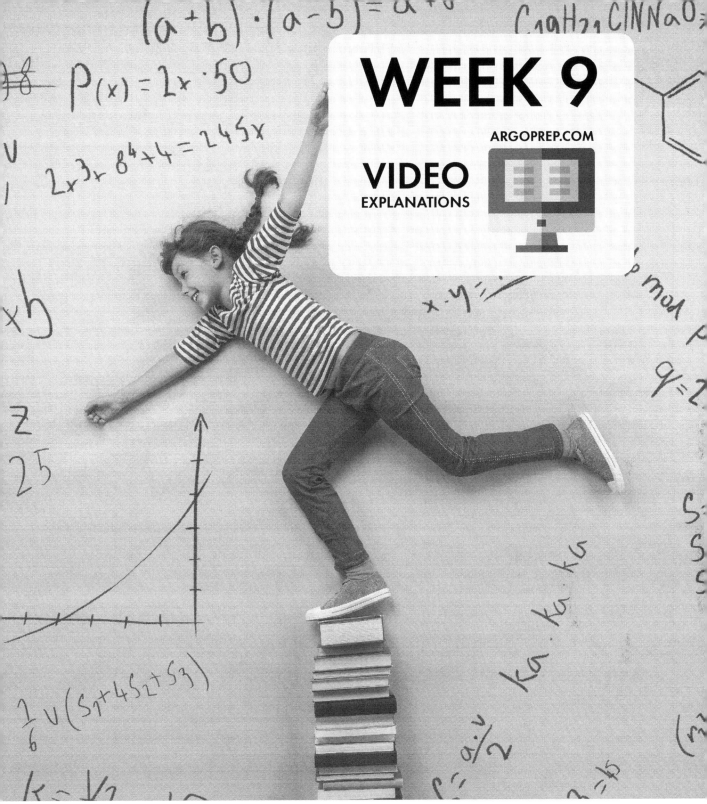

Statistics are the core of Week 9. You will practice finding and using random samples of a population. You will also begin to understand certain populations by gathering data and interpreting this data that reflects the given population.

You can find detailed video explanations to each problem in the book by visiting:
ArgoPrep.com

1. The music teacher wants to know which music class 8th grade students are most likely to take. What population would be the most representative?

7.SP.1

2. TV16 News Station wishes to know which sport is the most popular among its viewers. What population would be the best group to ask?

7.SP.1

3. A pet owners' magazine, *My Human*, wants to know which dog food most dog owners buy. What population would be the best group to ask?

7.SP.1

4. A caterer wishes to know the average number of guests that will be having dinner at a wedding reception. What population would be the best one to sample?

7.SP.1

5. What is the constant of proportionality for the table?

x	y
5	2.5
6	3
7	3.5

7.RP.2

6. Write an expression that is equivalent to $5a - 3 + 8b - 7a - b$.

7.EE.1

1. The principal at Hill Middle School wants to know how much time 7th grade students are spending on homework. What sample would be the most representative?

7.SP.1

2. Ms. Finnegan runs company TLLU and she donates some of its profits to charity. She wants to know which charity the majority of her employees would prefer. What population would be the best one to sample?

7.SP.1

3. Students in Mr. Hawkins' history class have to make and give a survey to find out the average age of people in their neighborhoods. What population would provide the most representative sample?

7.SP.1

4. A cake baker wishes to know the favorite cake flavor for groom cakes. Which population would be the best one to sample?

7.SP.1

5. The attendance monitor at Zippy's Preschool wants to know what time the 3 year old students wake up before coming to school. What sample would be most representative?

7.SP.1

6. A truckload of mulch can be used to fill $7\frac{7}{8}$ planters. A truckload weighs $3\frac{1}{2}$ tons. How many planters could 1 ton of mulch fill?

7.RP.1

DAY 3

If 5% of a population is surveyed and responds a certain way, then the total number of people likely to respond the same way is about 20 times the survey's result (because 5 X 20 = 100).

TIP of the DAY

---

1. Jamison randomly picked 10% of the soccer players in a league to ask them how many goals they scored. If 18 of the players said they scored 2 goals, what is the most reasonable prediction of the number of players who would say they scored 2 goals?

7.SP.2

---

2. If 20% of car drivers are surveyed and 42 of them say they have never had a ticket, what is the most reasonable prediction of the number of drivers who have never had a ticket?

7.SP.2

---

3. If 40% of the church attendees were surveyed and 18 of them said they were members, what is the most reasonable prediction of the number of church attendees who are members?

7.SP.2

---

4. When 25% of basketball players were asked how many games they played in last season, 23 of them said 12. What is the most reasonable prediction of the number of basketball players that played in 12 games last season?

7.SP.2

---

5. When 5% of moms were asked how much they spend on groceries each month, 236 of them said they spend $400 or more. What is the most reasonable prediction of the number of moms who spend $400 or more on groceries each month?

7.SP.2

---

6. What is the decimal equivalent of $\frac{32}{3}$?

7.NS.2

1. When 2% of adults at a concert were asked if they had a driver's license, 312 indicated they did. What is the most reasonable prediction of the number of adults at the concert that have a driver's license?

7.SP.2

Phone	Females	Males
Samsung	17	22
LG	12	11
iPhone	19	16
Alcatel	11	8

The chart shows the results of a school survey to see which phone brand most students used. **Use the table below to answer questions 2 – 4.**

2. Based on the survey, which phone did most students use?

7.SP.2

3. Based on the survey, which phone did most female students use?

7.SP.2

4. Based on the survey, which phone did the fewest number of students use?

7.SP.2

5. Four percent of teachers were asked how many hours they spent working at home. One thousand, four hundred sixty-two of them said more than 3 hours per night. What is the most reasonable prediction of the number of teachers that work more than 3 hours per night?

7.SP.2

6. Which property is shown below?

$(4m + 3n) + 8 = 8 + (3n + 4m)$

7.EE.1

Candidate	Females who would vote for	Males who would vote for
Fidelo	14	21
Garner	26	11
Lorelei	22	11
Kinley	17	15

The chart shows the results of a school survey to see who would be elected Treasurer of the Student Government. **Use the table given to answer questions 1 – 3.**

1. Based on the survey, who would most likely become Student Government Treasurer?

7.SP.2

2. Based on the survey, who would most likely receive the fewest votes?

7.SP.2

3. Based on the survey, if only boys voted, who would most likely win to become the treasurer?

7.SP.2

4. If 12.5% of the 7th graders were surveyed and 65 of them said they liked strawberry ice cream, what is the most reasonable prediction of the number of 7th graders who like strawberry ice cream?

7.SP.2

5. If 8% of the 8th graders were surveyed and 34 of them said Miss Bumpus was their favorite teacher, what is the most reasonable prediction of the number of 8th graders who have Miss Bumpus as their favorite teacher?

7.SP.2

DAY 6
CHALLENGE
QUESTION

Ten percent of students were surveyed about whom they would choose for Treasurer and the results are shown above in #1. Based on the Student Government table shown above, how many students were there?

7.SP.2

Now that you know and understand data sets, in Week 10 you will practice comparing and contrasting the information provided in data sets that may not look the same.

You can find detailed video explanations to each problem in the book by visiting:
ArgoPrep.com

DAY 1

Median is the middle number when the numbers are ranked from smallest to largest. For example, the median of 23, 24, 25, 37, 38, 40, 43 is 37.

TIP of the DAY

The number of fish per day that Jeffrey and Jonah caught over the past 12 days is shown below. **Use the information to answer questions 1 – 3.**

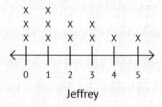
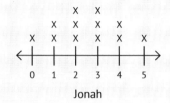

---

1. What is the range of Jonah's data set?

7.SP.3

---

2. Which boy has a higher mean of fish caught?

7.SP.3

---

3. What is the median of Jeffrey's data set?

7.SP.3

Jackie's swim times (in seconds) are shown below. **Use the information to answer questions 4 - 6.**

February	74	78	69	73	74
March	74	68	71	66	73

---

4. What is the difference between the medians of the 2 sets of scores?

7.SP.3

---

5. What is the difference between the means of the 2 sets of scores?

7.SP.3

---

6. What is the difference between the MAD of the 2 sets of data?

7.SP.3

There are 2 sisters who were preparing for a marathon. They went running each day for 20 days and their distances are shown below. **Use the information to answer questions 1 – 3.**

A	Distance Run (miles)						
0	7	8	9				
1	2	2	2	5	5	7	9
2	1	2	3	6	7		
3	0	3	4	4	5		

B	Distance Run (miles)					
0	2	3	3	5	5	7
1	2	3	3	6	8	9
2	3	5	6	7	8	9
3	1	1				

1. Which sister had (A) the lowest average distance and (B) by how much?

7.SP.3

2. Which sister had (A) the highest median distance and (B) by how much?

7.SP.3

3. What is the difference between the ranges of the 2 sets of data?

7.SP.3

Below are 2 data sets that show students growth in September of their 6th grade year and again their 8th grade year. **Use this information to answer questions 4 – 6.**

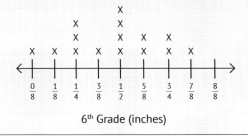

6th Grade (inches)

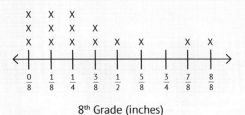

8th Grade (inches)

4. What is the difference in the medians of the 2 data sets?

7.SP.3

5. What is the difference in the ranges of the 2 data sets?

7.SP.3

6. What is the mean of the 8th grade data set?

7.SP.3

 **DAY 3**

MAD stands for the Mean Absolute Deviation.

Jerome's scores are shown below. **Use the information to answer questions 1 – 4.**

Economics	84	94	75	77	89	92	70
Psychology	95	80	85	90	88	86	92

1. What is the difference between the ranges of the 2 class scores?

7.SP.3

2. Which is the mean of the Economics scores data set?

7.SP.3

3. Which is the mean of the Psychology scores data set?

7.SP.3

4. What is the difference between the medians of the 2 class data sets?

7.SP.3

5. Last month Mrs. Thomas spent $60 on a pair of shoes. This month the same shoes are selling for $45. What is the percent decrease from last month to this month?

7.RP.3

6. Today Kevin worked on homework for $\frac{4}{5}$ of an hour in the morning, 6.3 hours in the afternoon and another 180 minutes in the evening. How much time did Kevin spend working on homework?

7.NS.3

TIP of the **DAY**

When working with statistics it is important to know the difference between range, median, mean and Mean Absolute Deviation (MAD).

DAY 4

The amount of rainfall (in inches) for 2 months is shown below. **Use the information given to answer questions 1 – 3.**

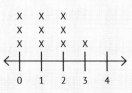

Rain (in inches) February

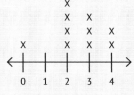

Rain (in inches) July

---

1. Using the table above, what is the difference between the means of the 2 data sets?

7.SP.3

---

2. Using the table above, which data set has the largest range and by how much?

7.SP.3

---

3. What is the MAD of February's rainfall?

7.SP.3

---

4. What is the median of July's data?

7.SP.3

---

5. Kevin could hike 21 km in $3\frac{1}{2}$ hours. How many km could he hike in $5\frac{1}{3}$ hours?

7.RP.1

---

6. A deposit for a cruise is $250. If you pay this month, you can receive a 10% discount. What will the deposit be if you pay this month?

7.RP.3

There were 2 elective classes and their scores are shown below. **Use the information from the data sets to answer questions 1 - 2.**

Spanish Scores							
7	2	7	8				
8	2	2	4	5	7	7	8
9	1	2	3	3	7		
10	0						

Art Scores						
7	2	3	5	7		
8	2	3	6	8	9	
9	3	4	5	7	8	9
10	0					

1. What is the difference in the ranges of the 2 sets of data?

7.SP.3

2. What is the mean of the Art scores?

7.SP.3

The temperatures over 8 days in January are shown below (in degrees Fahrenheit). **Use this information to answer questions 3 - 5.**

Florida	84	74	78	77	89	85	76	81
Michigan	45	30	51	47	48	56	50	42

3. Which state had the larger range and what is the difference between the ranges of the 2 data sets?

7.SP.3

4. What is the mean of the Florida temperatures?

7.SP.3

5. What is the median of the Michigan temperatures?

7.SP.3

DAY 6
CHALLENGE
QUESTION

Twenty percent of lawyers were polled. Forty-two of them said they worked more than 50 hours per week. What is a reasonable number that indicates how many lawyers work more than 50 hours per week?

7.SP.2

WEEK 11

Further building on what you've learned about data, Week 11 lets you use the data sets to find measures of center and measures of variability. These measures are then used to infer how a population might respond to a given scenario.

You can find detailed video explanations to each problem in the book by visiting:
ArgoPrep.com

 # DAY 1

Below are some measurements that were taken by Layla who grows flowers. She measured 2 types of flowers and charted the information. **Use the table below to answer questions 1 – 4.**

Number	Roses (inches	Lilies (inches)
1	18	32
2	16	25
3	21	28
4	19	24

1. Write a statement about the height of the 2 different types of flowers.

7.SP.4

2. What is the MAD of the rose data?

7.SP.4

3. What is the difference between the medians of the 2 data sets?

7.SP.4

4. What is the difference between the ranges of the 2 data sets?

7.SP.4

5. Altitude above sea level is given in positive values and below sea level is given in negative values. If Karissa started at 215 meters below sea level, increased her altitude by 1,732 meters before decreasing her altitude by 3,064 meters, what was her final altitude?

7.NS.1

TIP of the **DAY** *The range is the difference between the maximum and minimum in a data set and "mean" is the mathematical term meaning average.*

DAY 2

Below is a data set about the temperatures of 2 different cities. **Use the information to answer questions 1 – 4.**

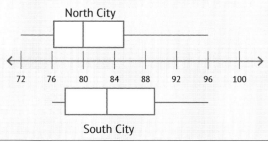

1. What is the range for North City?

7.SP.4

2. What is the difference between the medians in the 2 data sets?

7.SP.4

3. What is the range for South City?

7.SP.4

4. Write a statement about the medians of the 2 data sets.

7.SP.4

5. What fraction is equivalent to 0.375?

7.NS.2

6. If 4% of likely voters are surveyed and 159 of them say they would most likely vote for the Libertarian candidate, what is the most reasonable prediction of the number of voters who would chose the Libertarian candidate?

7.SP.2

The median is the middle number of a ranked data set that has an odd number of numbers.

Below are the scores for 2 of Lucy's classes – Spanish and Math. **Use the information provided to answer questions 1 – 4.**

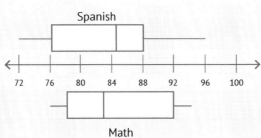

1. What is most likely the interquartile range for Lucy's Spanish grades?

7.SP.4

2. Write a statement comparing the median of the 2 classes.

7.SP.4

3. Which class has the least variance?

7.SP.4

4. What is most likely the difference between the ranges of the 2 data sets?

7.SP.4

5. The current taxes, *t*, on a home are expected to rise 3% next year. What will the taxes be after that increase?

7.EE.2

6. Write an expression that is equivalent to $(h - 5 - 3h) - 7 - (8h - 5h)$

7.EE.1

If a data set has an even number of numbers, the median is the average of the 2 middle numbers when the data is listed from smallest to largest..

DAY 4

Below are the votes for Student Body President by grade. **Use the table below to answer questions 1 – 4.**

Grade	Lance	Maggie
4	77	73
5	128	31
6	81	90
7	69	72
8	22	136

1. What is the difference between the means of the 2 sets of data?

7.SP.4

2. Who would most likely win the election and by how many votes?

7.SP.4

3. What grades are Lance and Maggie most likely in?

7.SP.4

4. Which candidate has the smallest MAD (Mean Absolute Deviation) and by how much?

7.SP.4

5. The Wagner's pool had a leak. It originally held 60,000 gallons but the leak caused it to lose 250 gallons of water each hour. How many gallons of water would remain after 1 full day?

7.NS.2

A record of one month's snowfall per day is shown below. **Use the information given to answer questions 1 – 4.**

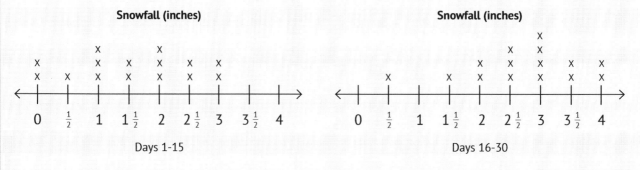

Snowfall (inches)

0 $\frac{1}{2}$ 1 $1\frac{1}{2}$ 2 $2\frac{1}{2}$ 3 $3\frac{1}{2}$ 4

Days 1-15

Snowfall (inches)

0 $\frac{1}{2}$ 1 $1\frac{1}{2}$ 2 $2\frac{1}{2}$ 3 $3\frac{1}{2}$ 4

Days 16-30

---

1. Which half of the month has a higher median and by how much?

7.SP.4

---

2. What is the difference between the ranges of the 2 sets of data?

7.SP.4

---

3. What is the (A) mean and (B) MAD of Days 1 – 15?

7.SP.4

---

4. What is the (A) mean and (B) MAD of Days 16 – 30?

7.SP.4

Monday	$6\frac{3}{4}$
Thursday	$6\frac{7}{8}$
Friday	$8\frac{1}{4}$
Saturday	$9\frac{3}{8}$

5. Kelli earns $16.52 per hour. The chart shows how many hours she worked last week. How much did Kelli earn last week?

7.EE.3

DAY 6
CHALLENGE
QUESTION

Using the snowfall data shown for numbers 1 – 4, what is the median for BOTH data sets combined? 7.SP.4

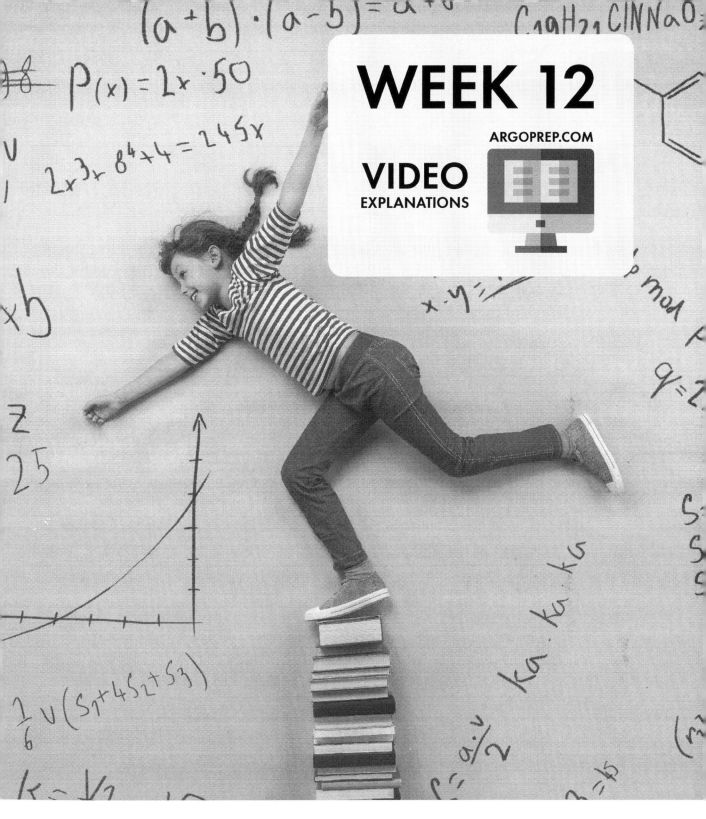

Are you interested in odds? If so, you will find Week 12 fun! This week you will be asked to use frequency to understand and approximate chance events by predicting and observing outcomes.

You can find detailed video explanations to each problem in the book by visiting:
ArgoPrep.com

DAY 1

The closer the probability of an event is to 1, the more likely it is that the event will occur.

1. Lewis is spinning a spinner. The probability that the spinner will land on 7 on his next turn is $\frac{1}{8}$. What word could be used to describe the probability that Lewis' next spin will be a 7?

7.SP.5

2. Francine the Fox is pregnant. What word could describe the probability that Francine will give birth to a fox?

7.SP.5

3. Katie has a box of marbles. The probability that she will randomly pick out a red marble on her next turn is $\frac{2}{3}$. What word could be used to describe the probability that Katie will pick a red marble next?

7.SP.5

4. Luca has a bag of coins. The probability that he will pick a jack is $\frac{0}{9}$. What word could be used to describe the probability that Luca will randomly select a jack?

7.SP.5

5. Below are some transactions that Karole made to her bank account.

Deposits	Withdrawals
203.15	869.98
419.57	210

If Karole's account had $856 before any deposits or withdrawals, what was her final balance?

7.NS.1

74

1. Lisa is spinning a spinner. The probability that the spinner will land on 1 on her next turn is $\frac{2}{7}$. What word could be used to describe the probability that Lisa's next spin will be a 1?

7.SP.5

2. David is kicking the ball into the goal. The probability that he will make the shot is $\frac{1}{5}$. What word could be used to describe the probability that David will score a goal?

7.SP.5

3. There is a 6-sided die that is numbered 1 – 6. What word describes the probability that Mia will roll a 7 on that die?

7.SP.5

4. Bennett is picking coins. There are 12 dimes, 8 nickels and 2 pennies. What word describes the probability that Bennett will pick a coin?

7.SP.5

5. Cutter is shooting baskets. The probability that he will make the shot is $\frac{7}{9}$. What word describes the probability that Cutter will make a basket?

7.SP.5

6. Rona the Rabbit is pregnant. What word describes the probability that Rona will give birth to a squirrel?

7.SP.5

DAY 3

An impossible event is one in which the desired outcome will never occur.

---

1. What fraction shows the probability that Martha will pick a red card from a standard 52-card deck?

7.SP.6

---

2. Micah has a toolbox that contains 9 wrenches, 8 screwdrivers, and 5 hammers. Write a fraction that can represent the probability that Micah will randomly pull a screwdriver from his toolbox.

7.SP.6

---

3. The probability of Meredith drawing a nickel from a bag is $\frac{1}{6}$. If she draws 1 coin at a time and replaces it, how many times would you expect Meredith to get a nickel if she tries 216 times?

7.SP.6

---

4. The probability of Phil making a hole-in-one is $\frac{1}{5}$. If Phil tries 345 times to get a hole-in-one, how many times would you expect Phil to get one?

7.SP.6

---

5. The probability of Max, a dog, pulling out a yellow sock from the laundry basket is $\frac{1}{7}$. If it randomly draws 1 sock at a time and its owner replaces the sock each time, how many times would you expect Max to pull out a yellow sock if he goes into the basket 735 times?

7.SP.6

---

6. There is a 5-sided die that is lettered A – E. What word describes the probability that Ken will roll a 5 on that die?

7.SP.5

TIP of the **DAY**

If the probability of an event is 3 in 5, it is said to have a probability of 3/5 or 0.6. It is a likely event.

DAY 4

Students will throw a cube onto an enclosed game board like the one shown below. **Use this game board to answer questions 1 – 3.**

1. What is the probability that Mason's cube will land on a white triangle?

7.SP.6

2. What is the probability that Mel's cube will land on a blue triangle?

7.SP.6

3. What is the probability that Lexi's cube will land on a yellow triangle?

7.SP.6

4. Write a fraction that shows the probability that Jay will pick a black club card from a standard 52-card deck.

7.SP.6

5. Write a fraction that shows the probability that Mona will roll a 3 on a fair die.

7.SP.6

6. Looking at the figure below, what is the probability of a coin landing on a white square?

7.SP.6

DAY 5 ASSESSMENT

1. There is a 6-sided die that is numbered 1 – 6. What word describes the probability that Lea will roll a number on that die?

7.SP.5

Below are 12 cups. One of them has a ball in it. **Use this information to answer questions 2 – 4.**

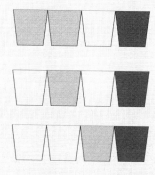

2. What is the probability that the ball is in a blue cup?

7.SP.6

3. What is the probability that the ball is in a yellow cup?

7.SP.6

4. What is the probability that the ball is in a cup?

7.SP.6

5. If the probability of Monique drawing a sapphire from a bag is $\frac{2}{11}$ and she draws 1 gem at a time and replaces it, how many times would you expect Monique to get a sapphire if she tries 187 times?

7.SP.6

6. Liz has a pocket of coins. The probability that she will randomly pick out a dime is $\frac{4}{9}$. Write a word that describes the probability that Liz will pick a dime.

7.SP.5

DAY 6
CHALLENGE
QUESTION

What is the probability that a person could randomly pick a yellow card from a deck containing 1 each of red, blue, yellow, green, black, and orange?

7.SP.6

Now that you understand a little bit more about probability and the likelihood of certain events, you can begin to create your own probability models using information you have been given.

You can find detailed video explanations to each problem in the book by visiting:
ArgoPrep.com

Probability models can be used to find the probability (or likelihood) for specific outcomes.

TIP of the **DAY**

There are 30 marbles in a bag and the number of each color is shown below. **Use the table to answer questions 1 – 3.**

Color	Number
Black	6
Red	2
White	5
Gray	7
Yellow	10

1. Based on the probability chart above, what is the probability that Les will draw out a yellow marble?

7.SP.7

2. Based on the probability chart above, what is the probability that Nelly will draw out a white marble?

7.SP.7

3. Based on the probability chart above, what is the probability that Nessa will draw out EITHER a red OR a gray marble?

7.SP.7

Neal has 20 socks in the clothes basket. Twelve of the socks are white and the rest are blue. Of the blue socks, 2 of them have stripes. **Use this information to answer questions 4 – 5.**

4. Based on the data, what is the probability that Neal will draw out a sock that has stripes?

7.SP.7

5. Based on the data, what is the probability that Neal will draw out a blue sock that does NOT have stripes?

7.SP.7

Color	Number
Orange	10
Pink	9
Green	13
Blue	11
Purple	7

There are 50 plastic coins in a box and the number of each color is shown on the chart. **Use the table below to answer questions 1 – 4.**

---

1. Based on the data given above, what is the probability that Calla will draw out a pink coin?

7.SP.7

---

2. Based on the data given above, what is the probability that Chaz will draw out a blue coin?

7.SP.7

---

3. Based on the data given above, what is the probability that Dru will draw out a green OR purple coin?

7.SP.7

---

4. What is the constant of proportionality for the table below?

x	y
2	5
3	7.5
10	25

7.RP.2

---

5. What is the decimal equivalent of $\frac{11}{12}$ rounded to the nearest thousandth?

7.NS.2

DAY 3

Probability is not a guarantee of a particular outcome; it merely states what the likelihood of a particular event is.

The students at RS Middle School were polled to see which club they would be most interested in. Fifty students were polled and their votes were placed into a jar that the principal will draw from to determine the new club. The responses are shown below. **Use the table below to answer questions 1 – 4.**

Class	Number
Pottery	15
Chinese	10
Frisbee	12
German	13

1. Based on the data, what is the probability that the principal will start a Chinese club?

7.SP.7

2. Based on the data, which club is the most probable one to be chosen?

7.SP.7

3. Based on the data, what is the probability that the principal will start a Frisbee club?

7.SP.7

4. Based on the data, what is the probability that the principal will start a club for foreign languages?

7.SP.7

5. If 25% of likely voters are surveyed and 317 of them say they would most likely vote for the youngest candidate for the office of City Organizer, what is the most reasonable prediction of the number of voters who would chose the youngest candidate for City Organizer?

7.SP.2

Minnie has a box of greeting cards and the number and type of card are shown below. **Use the table below to answer questions 1 – 4.**

Card	Number
Birthday	21
Sympathy	15
Wedding	9
New Baby	11
Retirement	4

---

1. Based on the data, what is the probability that Minnie would randomly draw a birthday card?

7.SP.7

---

2. Based on the data, what is the probability that Minnie would randomly draw a wedding card?

7.SP.7

---

3. Based on the data, what is the probability that Minnie would randomly draw a retirement OR a new baby card?

7.SP.7

---

4. Based on the data, what is the probability that Minnie would randomly draw any card EXCEPT a sympathy card?

7.SP.7

---

5. The number of letters sent via the postal service is expected to decrease by 8.1% in the next decade. If m represents the current number of mailed letters, write an expression that would represent the expected number of letters.

7.EE.2

Chicken Type	Eggs
Americana	4
Golden Comet	19
Leghorn	22
Rhode Island Red	5

Nikki raises chickens. She has eggs from different chickens and she keeps those eggs in her egg basket. The type of chicken and its number of eggs are shown. **Use the information given to answer questions 1 – 3.**

1. Based on the data, if an egg were randomly picked from the basket, what is the probability that Nikki would pick a Rhode Island Red egg?

7.SP.7

2. Based on the data, if an egg were randomly picked from the basket, what is the probability that Nikki would pick an egg from a Leghorn chicken?

7.SP.7

3. Based on the data, if an egg were randomly picked from the basket, what is the probability that Nikki would pick a Golden Comet OR an Americana egg?

7.SP.7

There are 100 apples in a bin. Thirty-five are Red Delicious, 32 are Fuji, 17 are Granny Smith and the rest are Gala apples. **Use this information to answer questions 4 – 5.**

4. If Marcel randomly picks an apple from the bin, what is the probability, as a decimal, that he will NOT pick a Gala apple?

7.SP.7

5. If Marcel randomly picks an apple from the bin, what is the probability, as a decimal, that he will pick a Red Delicious apple?

7.SP.7

DAY 6
CHALLENGE
QUESTION

There is a 4-sided die with numbers 1 – 4 on it. What is the probability that Matt will roll a 1 three times in a row?

7.SP.8

Did you find Week 13 pretty easy? This week you can step it up a notch. We are talking COMPOUND events this week! You can find these probabilities by using charts, diagrams, and simulations you create!

You can find detailed video explanations to each problem in the book by visiting:
ArgoPrep.com

1. Make a probability model that could show that Olivia had 2 pairs of shoes and 5 pairs of socks she could choose from.

7.SP.8

2. What is the probability that 4 coins thrown at the same time will all land tails?

7.SP.8

There are two 8-sided "dice" and each are numbered 1 – 8. **Use this information to answer questions 3 – 5.**

3. How many possible outcomes are there if both dice are thrown at the same time?

7.SP.8

4. What is the probability that both dice will roll an even number if they are both thrown at the same time?

7.SP.8

5. What is the probability that both dice will roll the same number?

7.SP.8

6. Find the value of the expression below.

5 − 36 + 19 − 38 + 49

7.NS.1

There is a 1 in 2 probability that a fair coin will land on heads when flipped in the air. There is also a 1 in 2 probability (0.5) that it could land on tails.

---

1. There are three "cubes" that have 7 sides each. Each side has 1 letter from A – G. What is the probability, as a fraction, that someone could get an A on each cube if thrown at the same time?

7.SP.8

---

2. There is one standard deck of cards. What is the probability that Leo could randomly draw a red card, replace it and then randomly draw an ace?

7.SP.8

---

3. Draw a probability model that could be used to show the probability of Ollie flipping a fair coin, then drawing a specific card twice from a deck of 3 cards labeled A, B and C, and then flipping another fair coin and getting a specific outcome on the coin.

7.SP.8

---

4. Using your probability model from above, what is the probability that Oliver will pick a "B" card twice and then roll a heads twice on the coin?

7.SP.8

---

5. What is the probability that Marcus can throw 2 fair coins and they land with tails on both?

7.SP.8

---

6. Hal has a nickel and 2 cubes that both have 8 sides. What is the probability that Hal can roll a heads on the nickel AND a 6 on the two cubes?

7.SP.8

**DAY 3**

The probability of flipping a tail on a fair coin is 1/2. The probability of getting heads on a fair coin three times in a row is 1/8 because 1/2 x 1/2 x 1/2 = 1/8.

1. There is one standard deck of cards. What is the probability that Laura could randomly draw an ace, replace it and then randomly draw a heart?

7.SP.8

2. Petra is going to fix an omelet. She can choose from 4 types of cheeses and 6 different vegetables. If she chooses 1 cheese and 1 vegetable, how many different combinations could she make?

7.SP.8

3. What is the probability of rolling 2 standard fair dice and having a sum of 7?

7.SP.8

There are 5 cards (each card is a different color), 1 six-sided die, and 3 coins. **Use this information to answer questions 4 – 6.**

4. What is the probability that Nick can roll a 3 on the die and pick a yellow card?

7.SP.8

5. What is the probability that Nick can get 2 heads on 1 coin thrown twice and roll a 1 on the die twice in a row?

7.SP.8

6. What is the probability that Nick can get 3 tails, a blue card and a 5 on the die?

7.SP.8

TIP of the **DAY**

It is impossible to get a "3" on a fair coin. The only 2 possible events are flipping a head or flipping a tail. The probability of getting a 3 on a fair coin is 0.

DAY 4

1. Draw a probability model that shows that Maddie had 3 notebooks and 4 pens from which she could randomly choose to write a story. The notebooks were white, orange or purple. The 4 pens were blue, black, red or green.

7.SP.8

2. Using the probability model you made above, what is the probability that Maddie will choose the purple notebook and the green pen?

7.SP.8

3. Using the probability model you made above, what is the probability that Maddie will choose the white OR orange notebook and the blue OR black pen?

7.SP.8

4. The probability that Morgan will score a goal is $\frac{1}{4}$. The probability that Miles will score a goal is $\frac{1}{5}$. What is the probability that both Morgan and Miles will score?

7.SP.8

5. What is the probability of rolling 2 fair dice and having the dice have a sum of 10?

7.SP.8

6. If the probability of Roxanne drawing a pearl from a bag of precious stones is $\frac{1}{8}$ and she draws 1 jewel at a time and replaces it, how many times would you expect Roxanne to get a pearl if she tries 280 times?

7.SP.6

Below is a list of the items that students have available to them. **Use this information to answer questions 1 – 3.**

Quantity	Item
2	Deck of 6 cards, each with a different color
3	5-sided cube lettered A – E
4	Fair coin (heads/tails)

1. What is the probability that Risha can get a tail using 1 coin and pick a yellow card from 1 deck and roll an A on 1 cube?

7.SP.8

2. What is the probability that Richie can roll tails on all 4 coins?

7.SP.8

3. What is the probability that Mallory can get 2 red cards, one coin that lands on heads AND three cubes that roll an E?

7.SP.8

4. Using a fair 7-sided die, numbered 1- 7, what is the probability that a person can roll a 6 three times in a row?

7.SP.8

5. Write an expression that is equivalent to $-8s + t - (-14s) + 9t + 5t$

7.EE.1

DAY 6
CHALLENGE
QUESTION

Using the items from questions 1 – 4, what is the probability that a person could get all heads on all coins, a D on all cubes and pick all orange cards in one try?

7.SP.8

90

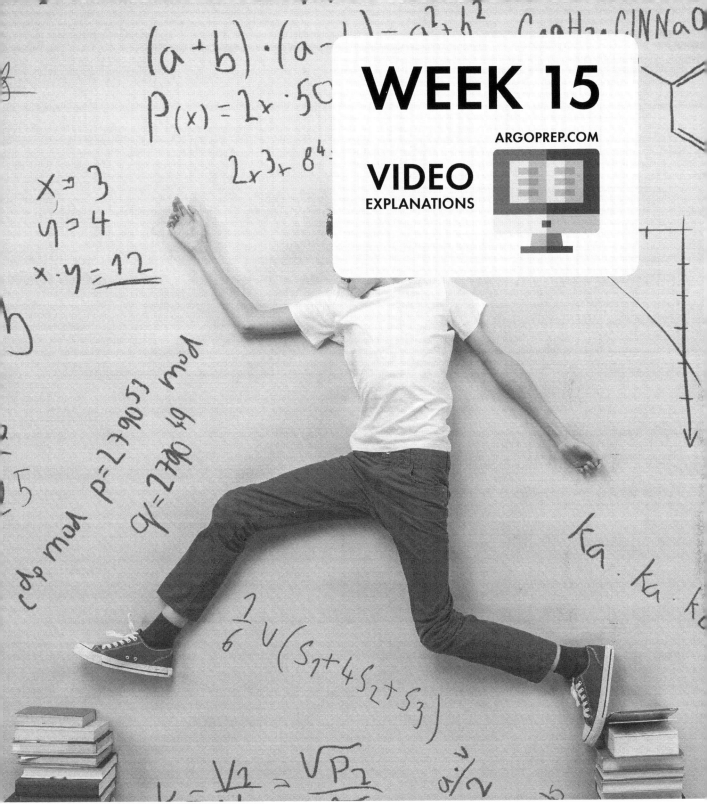

Have you ever wondered about being an architect or a construction worker?
In Week 15 we explore scale models and compare them to their actual rooms/buildings/heights.
This week you'll get practice working with blueprints and using scale models.

You can find detailed video explanations to each problem in the book by visiting:
ArgoPrep.com

 **DAY 1**

This week we are studying scale models. Remember that in a scale model, every dimension in the model is the same proportion to the corresponding dimension of the actual item.

 TIP of the DAY

1. The scale model of a car is 1 inch to 2.5 feet. If the real car is 12.5 feet, what is the length, in inches, of the model car?

7.G.1

The diagram below shows a model of a garage where each inch on the model is equal to 4 feet of the actual garage. **Use this figure to answer questions 2 – 3.**

Length: 9 inches

Width: 8 inches

2. What is the width, in feet, of the garage?

7.G.1

3. What is the length, in feet, of the garage?

7.G.1

4. The scale model of a stamp is 1 inch on the model to 3.5 mm on the actual stamp. If the model is 7.875 inches, what is the length, in mm, of the actual stamp?

7.G.1

5. If there is a die that has 12 sides, numbered 1 – 12, what is the probability that Sean will roll a 2, 7 or an 8?

7.SP.7

6. Which property is shown below?

$-3 (12 - 2c) = -36 + 6c$

7.EE.1

 of the DAY

You have finished 14 weeks of lessons – congratulations! Keep up the hard work and you will have learned a LOT that should help you on your tests!

DAY 2

---

1. The diagram below shows the dimensions of Kelsey's room. If a scale model were built so that 2 centimeters on the model represented 1 foot of the actual room, what would be the width, in centimeters, of the model?

Length: 10 feet

Width: 8 feet

7.G.1

---

2. The blueprint for a storage unit has a scale where 1.5 inches on the blueprint represents 2 feet on the actual storage unit. If the storage unit on the blueprint has a height of 12 inches, what is the height of the actual unit?

7.G.1

---

3. The blueprint of a playhouse has a key where 3 inches = 2 feet. If the playhouse on the blueprint is 9 inches tall, what is the height, in feet, of the actual playhouse?

7.G.1

---

4. The blueprint of a desk is 1 inch to 2.1 feet. If the actual desk is 8.4 feet long, what is the length, in inches, on the blueprint?

7.G.1

---

5. The teacher had $1\frac{2}{5}$ inches of mail on her desk when she left for the summer. While she was gone, the office placed her mail on her desk. If the mail pile grew by $\frac{3}{4}$ of an inch each day, how tall would the pile of mail be when the teacher returned after 13 days?

7.EE.3

---

6. What is the product of $\left(\frac{7}{4}\right) \times \left(-\frac{11}{7}\right)$?

7.NS.2

DAY 3

A scale model is often used to help us understand something that is either very large or very small.

The diagram below shows a scale model of the floor of a barn. The scale model is designed so that 1 cm on the model represents 7.2 feet on the actual barn. **Use this model to answer questions 1 – 2.**

Length: 7.5 cm

Width: 4 cm

---

1. What is the width, in feet, of the barn?

7.G.1

---

2. What is the length, in feet, of the barn?

7.G.1

---

3. The scale model of a boat is 1.5 inches to 2 yards. If the real boat has a cabin that is 20 yards, what is the length, in inches, of the model boat cabin?

7.G.1

---

4. If a tree is 30 feet tall and the model is 15 mm = 4 feet, what is the height of the model tree?

7.G.1

---

5. Altitude above sea level is given in positive values and below sea level is given in negative values. If Trevor started at 1,057 meters below sea level and increased his altitude by 2,435 meters before decreasing his altitude by 698 meters, what was his final altitude?

7.NS.1

---

6. What is the decimal equivalent of $\frac{150}{6}$?

7.NS.2

A scale model is not always smaller than the actual item. In science a model can be used to show something that is very small like a cell or DNA.

DAY 4

The diagram below shows a scale model of a cell. The scale model is designed so that 1 inch on the model represents 0.4 centimeters on the actual cell. **Use this model to answer questions 1 – 2.**

Length: 15 inches

Width: 10.5 inches

1. What is the length of the actual cell, in centimeters?

7.G.1

2. What is the width of the actual cell, in centimeters?

7.G.1

3. The scale model of a table is 1 inch to 0.8 feet. If the real table is 12 feet, what is the length, in inches, of the model table?

7.G.1

4. The blueprint of a chicken coop has a scale that is 5 cm to 3 feet. If the real coop is 8 feet tall, what is the approximate height, in cm, on the blueprint?

7.G.1

5. If a model has a scale where 3 cm on the model represents 1 meter on the actual item and the width of the item is 14 meters, what is the approximate length of the model?

7.G.1

6. There is a deck of 6 cards that are labeled 1 – 6. What is the probability that a player will draw a 4 three times in a row?

7.SP.8

DAY 5 ASSESSMENT

There is a 4-sided building that has a scale model where 4 inches on the model represents 7.5 feet of the actual building. **Use this information to answer questions 1 – 3.**

1. If a side on the scale model is 10 inches, what is the length of the corresponding side of the actual building?

7.G.1

2. If a side on the actual building is 22 feet, what is the approximate length of the corresponding side of the scale model?

7.G.1

3. If a side on the scale model is 15 inches, what is the approximate length of the corresponding side of the actual building?

7.G.1

4. The scale model of a train is 1 cm to 1.6 meters. If the actual caboose is 9.28 meters, what is the length, in cm, of the model caboose?

7.G.1

5. Below are some transactions that Sharon made to her bank account.

If Sharon's account had $32.56 before any deposits or withdrawals, what was her final balance?

Deposits	Withdrawals
291.83	314.88
425.76	487.90

7.NS.1

DAY 6 CHALLENGE QUESTION

There is a building that has a scale model where 2.5 cm on the model represents 4 feet on the actual building. If the length and the width of the actual building are 50 feet and 32 feet, what are the dimensions of the model building?

7.G.1

96

WEEK 16

Week 16 is all about triangles! You will have a chance to measure and determine the angle measures of triangles. You will also be able to identify specific types of triangles as well as other geometric shapes.

You can find detailed video explanations to each problem in the book by visiting:
ArgoPrep.com

The 3 angles in a triangle should have a sum of 180°.

TIP of the DAY

There are 4 shapes shown below. **Use this information to answer questions 1 – 3.**

Shape	Angle 1	Angle 2	Angle 3	Side 1	Side 2	Side 3
A	33°	110°	37°	9.5 in	16.4 in	10.5 in
B	97°	48°	35°	18 cm	9.7 cm	7.5 cm
C	32°	90°	58°	17 mm	32.1mm	27.2 mm
D	26°	107°	45°	19.5 ft	42.5 ft	32.5 ft

1. Which shape is a right triangle?

7.G.2

2. Which shape has angle measures that indicate it can NOT be a triangle?

7.G.2

3. Which shape has side lengths that indicate it can NOT be a triangle?

7.G.2

4. There is a triangle that has 2 angles that measure 15° and 151°. What is the measure of the third angle?

7.G.2

5. Write a factorization that is equivalent to $17jk + 51j$

7.EE.1

The 3 angles in an acute triangle all have measures less than 90 degrees.

DAY 2

---

1. There is a triangle that has 2 angles that measure 53° and 97°. What is the measure of the third angle?

7.G.2

---

2. There is a triangle that has 2 sides that measure 13.8 cm and 7.9 cm. The third side is the shortest side. Write a length that the third side would have to be in order for the figure to be a triangle.

7.G.2

---

3. There is a triangle that has 2 angles that measure 71.3° and 26.9°. What is the measure of the third angle?

7.G.2

---

4. There is a triangle that has 2 angles that measure 90° and 45°. What is the measure of the third angle?

7.G.2

---

5. You are to solve the equation: $16.8 = -4.2w$. What step should you take first?

7.EE.4

---

6. The scale model of a fireplace is 12 cm (model) to 1.5 feet (actual). If the actual fireplace is 9 feet, what is the approximate length, in cm, of the model?

7.G.1

DAY 3

Remember that when 2 sides of a triangle are added together, their sum must be greater than the length of the third side.

There are 4 shapes shown below. **Use this information to answer questions 1 – 3.**

Shape	Angle 1	Angle 2	Angle 3	Side 1	Side 2	Side 3
A	25°	126°	29°	7.9 in	18.1 in	9.1 in
B	72°	90°	18°	32.5 cm	34.2 cm	10.6 cm
C	104°	47°	30°	18.2 m	13.7 m	9.1 m
D	53°	74°	53°	17.3 in	20.8 in	17.3 in

1. Which shape is an isosceles triangle?

7.G.2

2. Which shape has side lengths that indicate it can NOT be a triangle?

7.G.2

3. Which shape has angle measures that indicate it can NOT be a triangle?

7.G.2

4. There is a triangle that has 2 angles that measure 12° and 97°. What is the measure of the third angle?

7.G.2

5. There is a triangle that has 2 angles that measure 69.4° and 92.1°. What is the measure of the third angle?

7.G.2

TIP of the DAY

You are ready for tomorrow's assessment. Be sure to have your tools at close reach.

DAY 4

1. There is a right triangle that has a side that is 45 degrees. How many degrees is the third angle?

7.G.2

2. There is a triangle that has 2 angles that measure 16.9° and 90°. What is the measure of the third angle?

7.G.2

3. There is a triangle that has 2 sides that measure 12.5 inches and 21.7 inches. The third side is the shortest side. Write a length that the third side would have to be in order for the figure to be a triangle.

7.G.2

4. There is a triangle that has 2 angles that measure 103.8° and 9.7°. What is the measure of the third angle?

7.G.2

5. If the probability of Kella drawing an orange card from a special deck of cards is 4/9 and she draws 1 card at a time and replaces it, how many times would you expect Kella to get a orange card if she tries 414 times?

7.SP.6

6. The buffet was priced at $1583. The store discounted it by 30% for 1 week. The next week they increased the price by 5%. What is the price now?

7.RP.3

There are 4 shapes shown below. **Use this information to answer questions 1 – 3.**

Shape	Angle 1	Angle 2	Angle 3	Side 1	Side 2	Side 3
A	63°	45°	72°	22.8 m	18.1 m	24.3 m
B	42°	90°	48°	15.6 in	23.3 in	17.3 in
C	12°	91°	87°	8.7 cm	31.8 cm	40.8 cm
D	102°	55°	23°	18.3 mm	15.3 mm	7.3 mm

1. Which shape has side lengths that indicate it can NOT be a triangle?

7.G.2

2. Which shape is an acute triangle?

7.G.2

3. Which shape has angle measures that indicate it can NOT be a triangle?

7.G.2

4. There is a triangle that has 2 angles that measure 10.3° and 58°. What is the measure of the third angle?

7.G.2

5. Using only one 7-sided cube, what is the probability that Vanessa will roll a 2 OR 5 on three straight rolls?

7.SP.8

DAY 6
CHALLENGE
QUESTION

There is a right triangle that has an angle that is 33 degrees. How many degrees is the 3rd angle of the triangle?

7.G.2

Have you ever cut a piece of wood and wondered about the shape that is made?
This week you will have lots of practice "cutting" open shapes and "seeing" how the shapes changed based simply on the way the shape is cut. Perpendicular and parallel cuts form different shapes than cuts that are not perpendicular or parallel.

1. Look at the cylinder shown. What shape is formed by the intersection of the plane and the cylinder?

7.G.3

2. Look at the sphere shown. What shape is formed by the intersection of the plane and the sphere?

7.G.3

3. If a cone is sliced with a plane that is perpendicular to its base and goes through the vertex, what shape is formed?

7.G.3

4. Look at the cube shown. What shape is formed by the intersection of the plane and the cube?

7.G.3

5. Look at the cone shown. What shape is formed by the intersection of the plane and the cone?

7.G.3

6. Jennifer poured $\frac{1}{2}$ a gallon of milk and it filled $\frac{3}{4}$ of a bottle. How many gallons would it take to fill the entire bottle?

7.RP.1

When asked to name a shape, be as specific as possible. Square and parallelogram are more specific than quadrilateral.

DAY 2

---

1. Look at the cylinder shown. It is "cut" by a plane that is neither parallel nor perpendicular to the bases. What shape is formed by the intersection of the plane with the cylinder?

7.G.3

---

2. Look at the cone shown. There is an intersecting plane that is parallel to the base of the cone. What shape is formed by the intersection of the plane and the cone?

7.G.3

---

3. If a pyramid is sliced with a plane that is parallel to its square base, what shape is formed?

7.G.3

---

4. Look at the pyramid shown. What shape is formed by the intersection of the plane and the pyramid?

7.G.3

---

5. Shown is a rectangular prism that has a rectangular base. If it were sliced by a horizontal plane, what shape would be created?

7.G.3

---

6. Raphael was able to make $\frac{1}{2}$ of the steak in 12 minutes. How many steaks could he make in 3 hours?

7.RP.1

DAY 3

When finding 2-dimensional shapes made from 3-dimensional shapes that are "cut" with a plane, make sure you check and see if the plane is parallel or perpendicular.

1. Look at the cylinder shown. What shape is formed by the intersection of the perpendicular plane and the cylinder?

7.G.3

2. Look at the sphere shown. What shape is formed by the intersection of the plane and the sphere?

7.G.3

3. If a horizontal slice of the figure shown is removed, what two-dimensional shape will the slice be?

7.G.3

4. If a pyramid is sliced with a plane that is perpendicular to its square base and goes through the vertex, what shape is formed?

7.G.3

5. Look at the cube shown. What shape is formed by the intersection of the plane and the cube?

7.G.3

6. The model of a nature center has a scale where 2 inches = 1.5 feet. If the model is 34 inches tall, what is the height, in feet, of the actual nature center?

7.G.1

No matter how a plane slices a sphere, if the plane goes completely through the sphere, the intersection will form a circle.

DAY 4

---

1. If a cone is sliced with a plane that is perpendicular to its circular base and goes through its endpoint, what shape is formed?

7.G.3

---

2. If a cone is sliced with a plane that is parallel to its circular base, what shape is formed?

7.G.3

---

3. Look at the cylinder shown. What shape is formed by the intersection of the plane and the cylinder? The plane is neither horizontal nor vertical to a base.

7.G.3

---

4. Look at the cube shown. What shape is formed by the intersection of the plane and the cube?

7.G.3

---

5. Look at the sphere shown. What shape is formed by the intersection of the plane and the sphere?

7.G.3

---

6. The blueprint for a school gymnasium has a scale where 3 inches on the blueprint represents 5 feet for the actual gym. If the gym on the blueprint has a height of 16.5 inches, what is the height of the actual gym?

7.G.1

1. Shown is a picture of a cylinder being sliced by a horizontal plane. What two-dimensional shape does this slice create?

7.G.3

2. There is a sphere that is sliced by a vertical plane. What shape is created by this slicing?

7.G.3

3. What shape is formed by the intersection of the pyramid shown and a non-horizontal plane? The base of the pyramid is a square.

7.G.3

4. The cone shown is being sliced by a horizontal plane. What two-dimensional shape is created at the intersection of the cone and the plane?

7.G.3

5. If a cube is sliced by a vertical plane, what shape is created?

7.G.3

6. What reduced fraction is equivalent to 0.0625?

7.NS.2

DAY 6
CHALLENGE
QUESTION

There is a rectangular prism that has 2 bases that both have 12 sides. If a plane parallel to the bases "cuts" the prism, what is the shape that is created?

7.G.3

Circles, circles, everywhere! In Week 18 you will be able to investigate the connection between a circle's area and its circumference. To extend your learning, you may be given the area and asked to find the circumference or vice versa.

You can find detailed video explanations to each problem in the book by visiting:
ArgoPrep.com

 **DAY 1**

The diameter of a circle is twice the circle's radius.

 **TIP** of the **DAY**

---

1. What is the radius, in cm, of a circle that has an area of 49π cm²?

7.G.4

---

2. The circumference of a circle is 24π inches. What is the area of the circle, in square inches? Express your answer in terms of π.

7.G.4

---

3. What is the diameter, in centimeters, of a circle that has a circumference of 10π centimeters?

7.G.4

There is information about 4 circles shown below. **Use the given information to answer questions 4 – 5.**

Circle A has a radius of 12 inches.
Circle B has a diameter of 15 inches.
Circle C has an area of 49π inches².
Circle D has a circumference of 10π inches.

---

4. Which circle has the largest area?

7.G.4

---

5. Which circle has the smallest diameter?

7.G.4

1. The mean radius of Binkley Park is 19 km and the mean radius of Downtown Park is 25 km. What is the approximate difference in the mean circumferences, in km, of the 2 parks? Round your answer to the nearest tenth of kilometer and use 3.14 for π.

7.G.4

2. The circumference of a circle is 11π inches. What is the area, in square inches, of the circle? Express your answer in terms of π.

7.G.4

There is information about 4 circles shown below. **Use the given information to answer questions 3 – 5.**

Circle W has a radius of 11 cm.
Circle X has a diameter of 16 cm.
Circle Y has an area of 144π cm².
Circle Z has a circumference of 7π cm.

3. Which circle has the smallest radius?

7.G.4

4. Which circle has the largest circumference?

7.G.4

5. Which circle has a perfect square (times pi) for its circumference?

7.G.4

6. There is a triangle that has 2 angles that measure 83° and 37°. What is the measure of the third angle?

7.G.2

DAY 3

To find the area of a circle, square the radius and then multiply by pi.

1. The mean radius of the cheese pizza is 5 inches and the mean radius of the supreme pizza is 8 inches. Using 3.14 for π, what is the approximate difference in the mean circumferences, in inches, of the 2 pizzas?

7.G.4

2. The diameter of a circle is 10 cm. What is the area, in square cm, of the circle? Express your answer in terms of π.

7.G.4

3. The area of the apple pie is 12.25π in² and the area of the cherry pie is 20.25π in². What is the difference in the radius of the 2 pies?

7.G.4

There are 4 circles shown below. Use π ≈ 3.14 and the diagram to answer questions 4 – 5. Round answers to the nearest hundredth when appropriate.

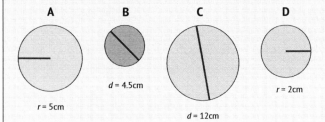

A   B   C   D

d = 4.5cm r = 2cm

r = 5cm d = 12cm

4. What is the circumference of Circle A?

7.G.4

5. What is the area of Circle C?

7.G.4

6. What two-dimensional shape is created by the intersection of the cylinder and the horizontal plane shown?

7.G.3

DAY 4

There is information about 4 circles shown below. **Use the given information to answer questions 1 – 3.** If necessary, use π ≈ 3.14

Circle 1 has a diameter of 8 meters.
Circle 2 has a radius of 6 meters.
Circle 3 has an area of 25π meters².
Circle 4 has a circumference of 16π cm.

1. Which circle has the largest area?

7.G.4

2. Which circle has a circumference of 25.12 meters?

7.G.4

3. Put the circles in order from the one that has the smallest area to the one that has the largest area.

7.G.4

4. What is the area, in mm, of a circle that has a diameter of 13 mm? Round your answer to the nearest hundredth of a square mm.

7.G.4

5. The mean circumference of the interstate bypass is 18π kilometers and the mean circumference of the actual interstate is 12π kilometers. What is the approximate difference between the 2 expressways' radii, in kilometers? Round your answer to the nearest hundredth of a kilometer.

7.G.4

6. Sunday morning it was −1.7°F. If the temperature dropped 2.3°F in the afternoon, what was the temperature in the afternoon?

7.NS.1

There is information about 4 circles shown below. **Use the given information to answer questions 1 – 3.**

Circle 5 has a diameter of 3 yards.
Circle 6 has a radius of 2 yards.
Circle 7 has an area of π yards².
Circle 8 has a circumference of 6π yards.

1. Which 2 circles have areas that differ by exactly 8π?

7.G.4

2. Which circle has the same circumference and area (but with different units)?

7.G.4

3. Put the circles in order from the one that has the smallest circumference to the one that has the largest circumference.

7.G.4

4. What is the area, in meters, of a circle that has a circumference of 24π meters? Leave your answer in terms of pi.

7.G.4

5. Velma earned $13.50 per hour. She got a new job in which she made 12% more. How much did she make per hour at her new job?

7.EE.3

6. Fifteen percent of 7th grade students are surveyed and 87 of them said their favorite color is blue. What number is the most reasonable prediction of the number of 7th grade students who would say blue is their favorite color?

7.SP.2

DAY 6
CHALLENGE QUESTION

Using the 4 circles from #'s 1-2 on this page, what is the total area of those 4 circles? Leave your answer in terms of π.

7.G.4

114

Sometimes people only look at things from one angle. Not in Week 19!
Here you can look at different kinds of angles like supplementary, complementary, adjacent and vertical angles. They are all special in their own way – check them out!

You can find detailed video explanations to each problem in the book by visiting:
ArgoPrep.com

 **DAY 1**

Supplementary angles are formed when 2 angles combine for a sum of 180°.

 **TIP** of the **DAY**

---

1. Two angles are supplementary. The first angle measures 50° and the second angle is 2x. What is the value of *x* in degrees?

7.G.5

The figure below is not to scale but can be used to answer questions 2 – 4. It is only shown to provide a visual of the relationship the angles have to each other.

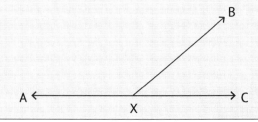

2. Angle AXC is 180°. If Angle AXB is 121°, what is the measure of Angle BXC?

7.G.5

---

3. Angle AXC is 180°. If Angle AXB is 149°, what is the measure of Angle BXC?

7.G.5

---

4. Angle AXC is 180°. If Angle CXB is 54°, what is the measure of Angle AXB?

7.G.5

---

5. Val is looking to rent a car. The info she found is shown below. Use the chart to find the 2 cars that have the same per day rental cost.

Car	Days	Cost
Compact	4	$174.00
Economy	3	$130.50
Intermediate	5	$225.00
Luxury	3	$153.00

7.RP.2

Use the figure below to answer questions 1 – 3. The diagram is not to scale and is only to be used as an aid to understanding an angle's relationship to other angles in the diagram.

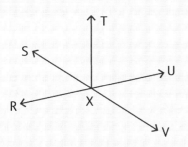

Angle SXV forms a straight angle and Angle UXR is also a straight angle. Angle RXS and Angle UXV are vertical angles.

---

1. If Angle SXR measures 52°, what is the measure of Angle UXV?

7.G.5

---

2. If Angle SXR measures 52°, what is the measure of Angle RXV?

7.G.5

---

3. If Angle RXV measures 143°, and Angle TXS measures 55°, what is the measure of Angle TXU?

7.G.5

---

4. Shown is a picture of a sphere being sliced by a plane. What two-dimensional shape does this slice create?

7.G.3

---

5. Veronica could run 21 km in 3 hours. How many km could she run in 5 hours?

7.RP.1

---

6. What is the value of the expression below?

531.7 – 204.58 – 418 + 619.88

7.NS.1

 **DAY 3**

When 2 lines intersect, they form vertical angles. Vertical, or opposite, angles are equal.

The figure below is not to scale but can be used to answer questions 1 – 3. It is only shown to provide a visual of the relationship the angles have to each other.

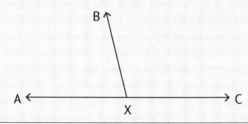

1. Angle AXC is 180°. If Angle AXB is 83°, what is the measure of Angle BXC?

7.G.5

2. Angle AXC is 180°. If Angle BXC is 111°, what is the measure of Angle AXB?

7.G.5

3. Angle AXC is 180°. If Angle CXB is 102°, what is the measure of Angle AXB?

7.G.5

4. Two angles are complementary. The first angle measures 20° and the second angle is 4m. What is the value of m in degrees?

7.G.5

5. Line DE intersects Line FG at Point H as shown below. What is the measure of Angle DHF?

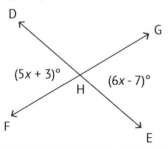

$(5x + 3)°$ $(6x - 7)°$

7.G.5

6. Write an expression that is equivalent to $5 (4c - 2) + (8 - 7c)$.

7.EE.1

Adjacent angles are angles that share a common ray and common vertex. Adjacent angles do not overlap.

DAY 4

Use the figure below to answer questions 1 – 4. The diagram is not to scale and is only to be used as an aid to understanding an angle's relationship to other angles in the diagram.
Line DE intersects Line FG at Point H.

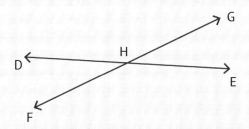

---

1. What type of angles are Angle DHF and Angle GHE?

7.G.5

---

2. What type of angles are Angle DHG and GHE?

7.G.5

---

3. If Angle DHF measures 37°, what is the measure of Angle GHE?

7.G.5

---

4. If Angle DHF measures 37°, what is the measure of Angle DHG?

7.G.5

---

5. Two angles are complementary. The first angle measures 45° and the second angle is 3*a*. What is the value of *a* in degrees?

7.G.5

---

6. An isosceles triangle has an Angle X that measures 58°. If Angle X is the smallest angle in the triangle, what is the measure of one of the other angles?

7.G.2

DAY 5 ASSESSMENT

1. Two angles are supplementary. The first angle measures 45° and the second angle is 5t. What is the value of *t* in degrees?

7.G.5

The figure shown is not to scale but can be used to answer questions 2 – 3. It is only shown to provide a visual of the relationship the angles have to each other.

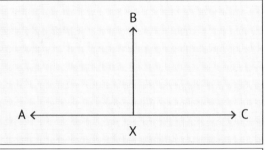

2. Angle AXC is 180°. If Angle AXB is 90°, what is the measure of Angle BXC?

7.G.5

3. What type of angles are Angle AXB and Angle BXC?

7.G.5

On the figure shown, Angle ACD is a straight angle. Angle DCB measures 127 degrees. **Use this information to answer questions 4 – 5.**

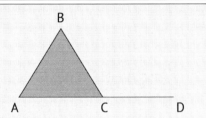

4. What is the measure of Angle BCA?

7.G.5

5. Using your answer from #4, what is the combined measure of Angles CAB and CBA?

7.G.5

6. Angle K and Angle L are complementary angles. If Angle K is 71°, what is the measure of Angle L?

7.G.5

DAY 6
CHALLENGE
QUESTION

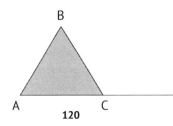

Angle A is 59° and Angle B is 61° as shown. What are the measures of Angles ACB and BCD?

7.G.5

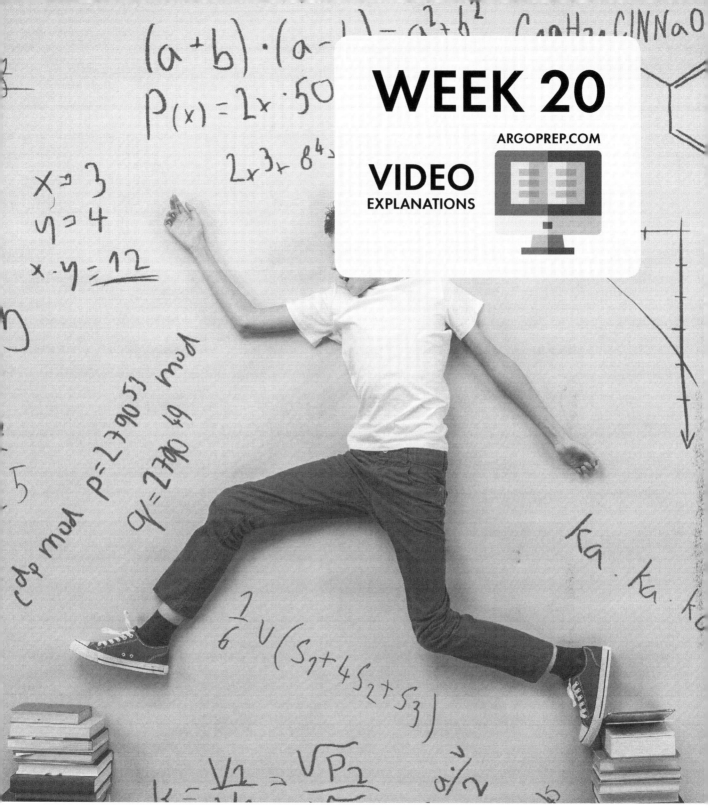

You have done a great job making it this far! Let's finish the workbook by finding the volume, surface area and area of two- and three-dimensional objects. You may need to "break them down" into smaller triangles, rectangles, squares or other quadrilaterals.

You can find detailed video explanations to each problem in the book by visiting:
ArgoPrep.com

 **DAY 1**

Volume can be found by multiplying the length, width and depth.

Use the rectangular solid shown to answer questions 1 – 3.

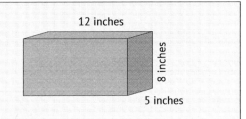

12 inches
8 inches
5 inches

---

1. How much space does the box above occupy?

7.G.6

---

2. If Xavier were to wrap the box with no overlap, how much wrapping paper would he need?

7.G.6

---

3. If Xavier stacked 6 boxes on top of each other, how much space would that column take up?

7.G.6

Use the figure shown to answer questions 4 – 5.

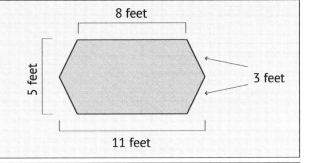

8 feet
5 feet
3 feet
11 feet

---

4. Above is a rug and Vince wants to know how much space it will take up on his floor. How much area does the rug cover?

7.G.6

---

5. Each rug is 3 inches thick. If Vince stacked 4 of the rugs on top of each other, what would be the volume of the 4 rugs?

7.G.6

---

6. An isosceles triangle is shown below. Angle E measures 38°. What is the measure of Angle G?

E

F   G

7.G.2

Use the figure shown to answer questions 1 – 3.

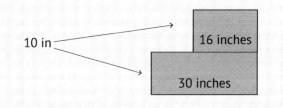

10 in

16 inches

30 inches

---

1. What is the total area of the figure shown above?

7.G.6

---

2. The steps shown above are 2 feet wide. What is the volume of the steps (in inches)?

7.G.6

---

3. What is the surface area of the steps above?

7.G.6

---

4. A triangle has a base of 5 inches and a height of 12 inches. If 6 of these triangles were put together to form a hexagon, what would be the area of the hexagon?

7.G.6

---

5. For the ancient Viking game of Kubb, there are 10 pieces of wood needed like the one shown. What is the total amount of wood required to play?

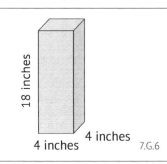

18 inches

4 inches

4 inches

4 inches

7.G.6

---

6. Which property is shown in the expression below?

$(5x + 3y) + 4z = 4z + (5x + 3y)$

7.EE.1

DAY 3

Area is measured in square units (cm², in², ft²) and volume is measured in cubic units (yds³, mi³, km³).

TIP of the **DAY**

Yancey had an old leather trunk that was 48 inches wide, 20 inches deep and 18 inches tall. **Use this information to answer questions 1 – 2.**

---

1. What is the volume of Yancey's box?

7.G.6

---

2. Yancey decided to recover the outside of the box with new leather. How much leather will he need?

7.G.6

Weston is building a fort like the one shown below. **Use the drawing of the fort to answer questions 3 – 4.**

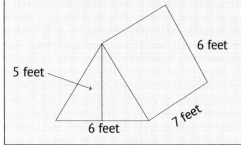

5 feet

6 feet

6 feet

7 feet

---

3. Since Weston does not need material for the floor, how much material will he need to make the fort?

7.G.6

---

4. How much space will Weston's fort occupy after he sets it up?

7.G.6

---

5. If a unit cube is 1 mm³ in volume, how many complete unit cubes would fit into a box that is 80 mm X 75 mm X 154 mm?

7.G.6

---

6. Two angles are supplementary. The first angle measures 33° and the second angle is 7y. What is the value of y in degrees?

7.G.5

1. There is a gift that Vanna has to give. It measures 18.5 cm by 12 cm by 22.5 cm. What is the volume of her gift?

7.G.6

2. Vanna wants to wrap the gift so that there is zero overlap on the wrapping paper. EXACTLY how much wrapping paper will Vanna need to wrap the gift?

7.G.6

3. If a unit cube is 1 cm³ in volume, how many complete unit cubes would fit into a box that is 155 cm X 49 cm X 105 cm?

7.G.6

4. What is the measure of Angle Z in the figure shown below?

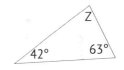

7.G.2

5. Line DE intersects Line FG at Point H as shown. What is the measure of Angle DHF?

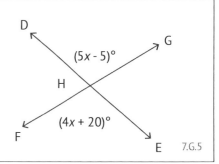

7.G.5

6. What is the decimal equivalent of $\frac{11}{3}$?

7.NS.2

DAY 5 ASSESSMENT

Use the figure shown to answer questions 1 – 2.

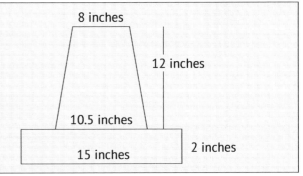

8 inches

12 inches

10.5 inches

15 inches

2 inches

1. What is the area of the figure shown above?

7.G.6

2. If the figure shown above were 4 inches thick, what would be its volume?

7.G.6

3. Each book measures 32.5 cm by 50 cm by 16.5 cm. If there are 15 books, how much space do they occupy?

7.G.6

4. If a unit cube is 1 in³ in volume, how many complete unit cubes would fit into a box that is 18.5 in X 25 in X 20 in?

7.G.6

5. What is the probability that a person could roll an even number on 3 straight rolls of a fair die?

7.SP.8

6. Zena randomly picked 12.5% of the 7th graders and asked them their favorite color. If 35 of the students said purple, what is the most reasonable prediction of the number of 7th grade students who would choose purple as their favorite color?

7.SP.2

DAY 6
CHALLENGE QUESTION

What are some ways you can "break apart" this hexagon to find its area?

7.G.6

THE END!

Assessment

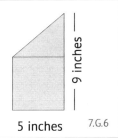

ASSESSMENT

There are 60 marbles in a bag and the number of each color is shown below. **Use the table below to answer questions 1 – 2.** Answers should be written as reduced fractions.

Color	Number
White	5
Clear	8
Silver	11
Blue	21
Red	15

1. Based on the data, what is the probability that Ted will draw out a blue marble?

7.SP.7

2. Based on the data, what is the probability that Ana will draw out a silver OR a red marble?

7.SP.7

3. Below is a trapezoid made up of a square and a triangle. What is the area of the trapezoid?

9 inches

5 inches   7.G.6

4. Name the property that is shown below.

$(4a + 6b) + 3c = 3c + (6b + 4a)$

7.EE.1

5. What is the constant of proportionality for the table below?

x	y
2	6
5	15
3	9

7.RP.2

6. There are 2 eight-sided fair dice. How many possible outcomes are there if both dice are thrown at the same time?

7.SP.8

7. The circumference of a circle is 32π inches. What is the area, in square inches, of the circle? Express your answer in terms of π.

7.G.4

8. Convert $\frac{7}{9}$ to its decimal equivalent using long division.

7.NS.2

9. Cathy was able to plant $2\frac{4}{5}$ rows of beans in 12 minutes. How many rows could Cathy plant in an hour?

7.RP.1

10. Wyatt is spinning a spinner. The probability that the spinner will land on an odd number on his next turn is $\frac{2}{3}$. Which word could be used to describe the probability that Wyatt's next spin will be an odd number?

7.SP.5

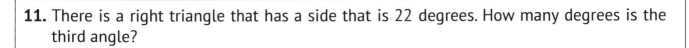

11. There is a right triangle that has a side that is 22 degrees. How many degrees is the third angle?

7.G.2

12. Five students bought some school supplies to share. Each package of school supplies was $3.95. They bought 8 packages of school supplies. If they also shared the price, how much money would each student give?

7.NS.3

13. A recliner that regularly sells for $798 was on sale for 35% off the regular price. What is the sale price?

7.EE.3

14. A triangle has a base of 12 inches and a height of 5 inches. If 6 of these triangles were put together to form a hexagon, what would be the area of the hexagon?

7.G.6

15. If the probability of Phoenix drawing a green marble from a pouch is $\frac{5}{9}$ and she randomly draws 1 marble at a time and replaces it, how many times would you expect Phoenix to get a green marble if she tries 117 times?

7.SP.6

16. Use the figure below where Angle AXC is 180°. If Angle AXB is 118°, what is the measure of Angle BXC?

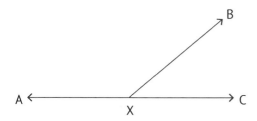

7.G.5

17. At the amusement, an adult ticket is $38.95, a children's ticket is $24.50 and a senior ticket is $29. The Nicola family is taking 7 adults, 12 children and 3 seniors to the park. What is the total cost for their tickets?

7.NS.3

18. The diagram below shows the dimensions of an area rug that Bonita cut out. If Bonita cut out a piece of material that was a scale model of the rug and 4.5 cm on the model represented 2 feet on the actual rug, what would be the dimensions of the material Bonita cut?

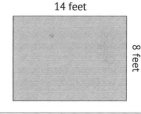

14 feet

8 feet

7.G.1

19. What is the product of $\left(\frac{3}{5}\right) \times \left(-\frac{5}{3}\right)$?

7.NS.2

20. The radio station played 300 songs on Friday. On Saturday, the station played 20% more songs than on Friday. Monday they played 5% fewer songs than on Saturday. How many songs did the station play on Monday?

7.RP.3

ASSESSMENT

21. Below are some transactions (in dollars) that Logan made to his bank account.

Deposits	Withdrawals
302.85	- 546.12
719	- 215.79

If Logan's account had $425.37 before any deposits or withdrawals, what was his final balance?

7.NS.1

22. There is a triangle that has 2 angles that measure 81° and 19°. What is the measure of the third angle?

7.G.2

23. Charlotte earns $25 for the first 8 students she gets to sign up for a tutor. She then makes $32.50 for every student after that. If Charlotte was able to sign up 22 students, how much would she earn?

7.EE.3

24. Bree ran 26 km in 3 hours. How far could Bree run in 5 hours?

7.RP.1

25. Altitude above sea level is given in positive values and below sea level is given in negative values. If Alex started at 1,500 meters below sea level and decreased his altitude by 1,675 meters before increasing his altitude by 3,249 meters, what was his final altitude?

7.NS.1

26. Look at the rectangular prism shown. It has 4 sides that are rectangles and 2 sides (the bases) that are squares. A horizontal plane "cuts" the prism. What shape is formed by the intersection of the plane and the prism?

7.G.3

27. The mean radius of Patriots Park is 10 km and the mean radius of Lions Park is 7 km. What is the approximate difference in the mean circumferences, in km, of the 2 parks? Answers have been rounded to the nearest hundredth of a km.

A. 9.42 km

B. 18.84 km

C. 21.98 km

D. 25.12 km

7.G.4

28. Rose took some measurements of her flowers. The information is charted below. Use the table below to answer the question.

Number	Sunflowers (inches)	Clematis (inches)
1	62	36
2	59	21
3	65	38
4	58	28

Which statement is NOT true about the flowers that were measured?

A. The sunflowers have a higher mean than the clematis.

B. The MAD of the sunflowers is 2.5.

C. The median of the clematis is 32.

D. The range is larger for the sunflowers than for the clematis.

7.SP.4

29. If 20% of 7th graders are surveyed and 28 of them say that Mrs. Deaton is the best teacher, what is the most reasonable prediction of the number of 7th graders who would vote for Mrs. Deaton as Teacher of the Year?

A. 6

B. 56

C. 140

D. 280

7.SP.2

ASSESSMENT

30. Sherri's first nursing exam score was a 150. After she retook the exam her score was 125. What is the percent decrease from the first test to the second test?

A. 17%
B. 20%

C. 80%
D. 83%

7.RP.3

31. Melody starts with $14. She earns 17 dollars for each babysitting job she has. Which equation shows how many dollars, D, that Melody has after B babysitting jobs?

A. $D = 31B$
B. $D = 17B - 14$

C. $D = 14B + 17$
D. $D = 17B + 14$

7.EE.4

32. The probability that Garrett will pick a green card is $\frac{2}{5}$. The probability that Nate will pick a yellow card is $\frac{1}{3}$. What is the probability that Garrett will pick a green card and Nate will pick a yellow card?

A. $\frac{1}{5}$

B. $\frac{2}{8}$

C. $\frac{3}{8}$

D $\frac{2}{15}$

7.SP.8

33. Nora bought a pair of socks that were discounted $18\frac{1}{5}$ %. If the non-sale price was s, which expression represents the cost Nora paid for the socks?

A. $s - 0.182s$
B. $1 - 0.818s$

C. $1.182s$
D. $s - 0.818$

7.EE.2

34. The scale model of a train is 2 cm to 1.5 feet. If the real engine car on the train is 61.5 feet, what is the length, in cm, of the model engine car?

A. 41 cm
B. 65 cm

C. 82 cm
D. 130 cm

7.G.1

35. Ariella has a jewelry box of rings. The probability that she will randomly pick out an onyx ring is $\frac{3}{8}$. Which statement describes the probability that Ariella will pick an onyx ring?

A. likely

B. certain

C. unlikely

D. impossible

7.SP.5

---

36. You are to solve the equation: $16.8 = -8.4r$. What step should you take first?

A. Add −8.4

B. Subtract −8.4

C. Multiply by −8.4

D. Divide by −8.4

7.EE.4

---

37. Watermelons cost $0.39 per pound. What equation is used to find C, the total cost for p pounds of watermelon?

A. $C = 0.39 + p$

B. $C = 0.39p$

C. $C + 0.39 = p$

D. $0.39C = p$

7.RP.2

The number of boxes of cookies sold by members of 2 Cookie Scout troops is shown. **Use the information to answer questions 38 – 39.**

Troop A	42	38	35	71	59	49	41
Troop B	56	35	41	38	27	30	45

---

38. Which statement is true about Troops A and B's numbers?

A. Troop A had a lower range than Troop B.

B. Troop A's median is 4 more than Troop B's median.

C. Troop B's mean absolute deviation (MAD) is about 3 more than Troop A's MAD.

D. Troop B's scouts sold more boxes of cookies than Troop A's scouts.

7.SP.3

---

39. What is the approximate difference between the means of the 2 troop numbers?

A. 5

B. 7

C. 8

D. 9

7.SP.3

ASSESSMENT

---

40. Which expression represents a factorization of $125xyz - 55xy + 5x$?

   A. $5x(25yz - 11)$
   B. $5x(120xyz - 11y) + 1$
   C. $5x(25yz - 11y + 1)$
   D. $5x(120yz - 50y)$

7.EE.1

---

41. Two angles are complementary. The first angle measures 24° and the second angle is $6w$. What is the value of w in degrees?

   A. 11°
   B. 26°
   C. 66°
   D. 156°

7.G.5

---

42. The new basketball coach wants to know which players are likely to shoot and make 3- point shots. Which population would be the best group to ask?

   A. every 4th cheerleader who went to the games last year
   B. every 6th baseball player who had the highest batting averages
   C. every 5th person who sold snacks in the concession stand last year
   D. every 3rd person who was on the basketball team last year

7.SP.1

---

43. Jay wants to purchase a canoe for $512. Each month he is able to save $38 for the purchase. If he has $125 already set aside, how many months will it take Jay to save enough money to buy the canoe?

   A. 9
   B. 10
   C. 11
   D. 12

7.EE.4

ANSWER
KEYS

VIDEO
EXPLANATIONS

ARGOPREP.COM

ANSWER KEY

For more practice with 7th Grade Math, be sure to check out our other book, Common Core Math Workbook Grade 7: Multiple Choice

WEEK 1

Day 1
1: −17.27
2: − 37meters
3: −$70 − $24 = −$94
4: $332.69
5: −16.3°F

Day2
1: 828 feet
2: $237.50
3: $106 − $50 − $12
4: 63.8°F
5: − 29 yards
6: −31

Day 3
1: 5°C
2: $929.46
3: − 425 feet
4: 58.89
5: 24.6°
6: −12.1°C

Day 4
1: 0.375
2: $-\frac{3}{20}$
3: $0.1\overline{6}$ or 0.1666...
4: $0.\overline{8}$ or 0.888...
5: $-\frac{2}{3}$
6: 23 − 18 or 23 + (− 18)

Day 5
1: $546.21
2: − 256 feet
3: 11 − 17 or 11 + (−17)
4: $0.\overline{63}$ or 0.6363...
5: 0.4

Day 6
−1.5°C

WEEK 2

Day 1
1: 0.369
2: 0.8
3: $\frac{21}{32}$
4: 0.875
5: $-\frac{3}{14}$
6: $503.34

Day 2
1: 3.25
2: $\frac{11}{32}$
3: − 144.65
4: 0.65
5: 0.6
6: 343 yards

Day 3
1: 62 inches
2: 65.9 miles
3: $40.25
4: $82.80
5: $12.45
6: −2.6°C

Day 4
1: − 962 feet
2: 350 miles
3: 25 hours
4: $756
5: 15.4 hours
6: 3,925 plants

Day 5
1: $19,004
2: $9,723.50
3: 149 − 57 + 23 = 115
4: 3.4 hours or 3 hours and 24 minutes
5: 66.4°F
6: $\frac{-14}{45}$

Day 6
$2,469

WEEK 3

Day 1
1: 12b (2a− 1)
2: Commutative Property
3: 10x +3
4: 7d (15+ 11e)
5: 21.24
6: 4h + 7

Day 2
1: Commutative Property
2: 4k (9j − 8)
3: 6e − 5
4: Distributive Property
5: Commutative Property
6: 4x + (9x +12x)

Day 3
1: Distributive Property
2: Commutative Property
3: 20c − 9
4: 25st (5+ 2r)
5: −8.0°C

Day 4
1: 16x (4yz − 2y + z)
2: Distributive Property
3: $-\frac{20}{27}$
4: 10.3m − 8.5n
5: 6sq − 10qrs + 8pqs
6: 0.25

Day 5
1: 12.3p − q
2: 30abc + 25abd − 50abe
3: Associative Property
4: Distributive Property
5: $\frac{3}{5}u + 3v - \frac{21}{5}w$

Day 6
7a (8 − 2b + 3c)

WEEK 4

Day 1

1: $c + 0.08c$ or $1.08c$
2: The length is 5 times the width.
3: The perimeter is 12 times the width.
4: $d - 0.13d$ or $0.87d$
5: 2.0
6: $e + 0.095e$ or $1.095e$

Day 2

1: $0.8s$ or $s - 0.2s$

2: The length is $\frac{1}{4}$ the width.

3: The perimeter is 2.5 times the width.
4: $15x - 16y$

5: $g + 0.43g$ or $1.43g$

6: 32/45

Day 3

1: $t + 0.065t$ or $1.065t$
2: The height is 4 times the width.
3: The perimeter is 10 times the width.
4: $-6b$
5: $0.75b$ or $b - 0.25b$
6: $526.34

Day 4

1: The length is 6 times the width.
2: The perimeter is 14 times the width.
3: $v + 0.52v$ or $1.52v$
4: $0.96w$ or $w - 0.04w$
5: $0.93p$ or $p - 0.07p$
6: Associative Property

Day 5

1: $c + 0.1175c$ or $c + 1.1175c$
2: $7a (2x + 5y - 4z)$
3: $0.952b$ or $b - 0.048b$
4: The perimeter is 8 times the width.

5: The width is $\frac{1}{3}$ the height.

6: $t + 0.135t$ or $1.135t$

Day 6

$0.75p$ or $p - 0.25p$

WEEK 5

Day 1

1: $13.35
2: 5°C
3: $29.25

4: $4\frac{1}{2}$ inches

5: $8f - g$
6: $58.50

Day 2

1: 0
2: $292.19
3: $0.22
4: 11 pounds
5: Commutative Property

Day 3

1: $372.94
2: −$0.94

3: $5\frac{1}{8}$ pounds

4: $22.73
5: 8.2%

Day 4

1: Space #8

2: $\frac{3}{4}$ of an inch

3: 280 hours

4: $94\frac{1}{2}$ yards

5: -25/49

Day 5

1: $690.37
2: $592.71

3: $6\frac{1}{8}$

4: $3.35

5: $3\frac{3}{20}$

6: 1.375

Day 6

$21\frac{3}{4}$ meters

WEEK 6

Day 1

1: $F = 7M + 33$
2: 9 months
3: 21 blocks
4: $P = a + 8 + 8 + 5$
5: $t > 4$
6: 8%

Day 2

1: $P = A + B + C + D + 8$
2: $P = 4 \times 13$
3: $d \geq -12$
4: $m = 15h - 24$

5: $\frac{16}{35}$

6: $1.9a - 10b + 23.6$

Day 3

1: 6 days
2: Add 6
3: 90 inches
4: 7 weeks
5: $0.875r$ or $r - 0.1125r$
6: $562w + 231 = D$

Day 4

1: 21 months
2: $2w = 210 - 114$
3: Add 5
4: $525.75
5: $14.85

Day 5

1: $P = A + B + C + 18$
2: Subtract 7
3: 34 mm
4: $12.5
5: $d + 0.085d$ or $1.085d$

Day 6

$P = 12.57f - 1.08f$ or $P = 11.49f$

WEEK 7

Day 1
1: $1\frac{1}{2}$

2: 30

3: $26\frac{2}{5}$

4: $28\frac{7}{8}$ km

5: $3\frac{1}{2}$ yds²

6: Divide by $\frac{2}{3}$ or multiply by $\frac{3}{2}$

Day 2
1: 13 tons

2: $23\frac{1}{3}$ rows

3: $2\frac{1}{7}$ pounds

4: $6\frac{3}{5}$ dressers

5: 8 miles

6: 19 lawns

Day 3
1: $\frac{12}{11}$ or $1\frac{1}{11}$ of a gallon

2: 2

3: A

4: C

5: B

Day 4
1: $C = 8.97t$

2: $\frac{1}{2}$

3: D

4: 1

5: C

Day 5
1: $\frac{1}{5}$

2: $C = 2.84a$

3: 3

4: 6m²

5: C and D

Day 6
2

WEEK 8

Day 1
1: 1,944 books

2: 20%

3: $22

4: $2,728.44

5: 48.6°F

6: $p + 0.073p$ or $1.073p$

Day 2
1: 60%

2: 30%

3: $17.64

4: 36%

5: 12.5%

6: -18/11

Day 3
1: $201.25

2: 75.6

3: 25%

4: 100%

5: 23.558

Day 4
1: $559.35

2: 105.84 inches

3: 50%

4: $887.40

5: $1,525.66

6: 7.5

Day 5
1: 50%

2: 400%

3: 80%

4: 31.5 mm

5: $59.99

6: Distributive Property

Day 6
Aiden decreased his time by 10% and Charity decreased her time by 20%. Charity had the larger percent of decrease.

WEEK 9

Day 1
1: A population that randomly chooses from among all 8th graders

2: A population that randomly chooses people who watch TV16 News Station

3: A population that randomly chooses people purchasing dog food

4: A population that randomly chooses brides/grooms

5: $\frac{1}{2}$

6: $-2a + 7b - 3$

Day 2
1: A sample that randomly chooses 7th grade students from Hill Middle School

2: A random sample of TLLU employees

3: A random sample of people from the students' neighborhoods

4: A population that randomly chooses grooms

5: A random sample of the parents of 3 year old Zippy students

6: $2\frac{1}{4}$

Day 3
1: 180

2: 210

3: 45

4: 92

5: 4,720

6: 10.666...

Day 4
1: 15,600

2: Samsung

3: iPhone

4: Alcatel

5: 36,550

6: Commutative Property

Day 5
1: Garner

2: Kinley

3: Fidelo

4: 520

5: 425

Day 6
1,370

WEEK 10

Day 1
1: 5
2: Jonah
3: 1.5
4: 3
5: 3.2
6: 0.64

Day 2
1: Sister B by 3.75 miles
2: Sister A by 3 miles
3: 1
4: $\frac{1}{4}$ inch
5: $\frac{1}{8}$ inch
6: 0.325 inches

Day 3
1: 9
2: 83
3: 88
4: 4
5: 25%
6: 10.1 hours or 10 hours and 6 minutes

Day 4
1: 1.3
2: July has 1 more in its range than February
3: 0.84
4: 2.5
5: 32
6: $225

Day 5
1: 0
2: 87.56
3: Michigan, 11
4: 80.5° F
5: 47.5° F

Day 6
210 lawyers

WEEK 11

Day 1
1: The lilies tend to grow about 8-9 inches taller than the roses
2: 1.5
3: 8
4: 3
5: −1,547 meters

Day 2
1: 24
2: 3
3: 20
4: North City has a lower median than South City
5: $\frac{3}{8}$
6: 3,975

Day 3
1: 12
2: The Spanish class has a median that is about 2 points higher than the median of the Math class.
3: Math
4: 6
5: 1.03t or t + 0.03t
6: −5h − 12

Day 4
1: 5
2: Maggie would win by 25 votes.
3: Most likely Maggie is in 8th grade and Lance is in 5th grade.
4: Lance by 2.16
5: 54,000 gallons

Day 5
1: Days 16 – 30 have a median that is 1.5 inches more.
2: $\frac{1}{2}$ inch
3: A. 1.5666... B.0.80444...
4: A. 2.7 B.0.72
5: $516.25

Day 6
$2\frac{1}{4}$ inch

WEEK 12

Day 1
1: unlikely
2: certain
3: likely
4: impossible
5: $398.74

Day 2
1: unlikely
2: unlikely
3: impossible
4: certain
5: likely
6: impossible

Day 3
1: $\frac{1}{2}$
2: $\frac{4}{11}$
3: 36
4: 69
5: 105
6: impossible

Day 4
1: $\frac{1}{3}$
2: $\frac{1}{9}$
3: $\frac{5}{9}$
4: $\frac{1}{4}$
5: $\frac{1}{6}$
6: $\frac{5}{12}$

Day 5
1: certain
2: $\frac{1}{4}$
3: $\frac{1}{3}$
4: $\frac{12}{12}$
5: 34
6: unlikely

Day 6
$\frac{1}{6}$ or 0.1666...

WEEK 13

Day1
1: $\frac{1}{3}$
2: $\frac{1}{6}$
3: $\frac{3}{10}$
4: $\frac{1}{10}$
5: $\frac{3}{10}$

Day2
1: $\frac{9}{50}$
2: $\frac{11}{50}$
3: $\frac{2}{5}$
4: 2.5
5: 0.917

Day 3
1: $\frac{1}{5}$
2: Pottery
3: $\frac{6}{25}$
4: $\frac{23}{50}$
5: 1,268

Day 4
1: $\frac{7}{20}$
2: $\frac{3}{20}$
3: $\frac{1}{4}$
4: $\frac{3}{4}$
5: $m - 0.081m$ or $0.919m$

Day 5
1: $\frac{1}{10}$
2: $\frac{11}{25}$
3: $\frac{23}{50}$
4: 0.84
5: 0.35

Day 6
$\frac{1}{64}$

WEEK 14

Day 1
1:

2: $\frac{1}{16}$
3: 64
4: $\frac{1}{4}$
5: $\frac{1}{8}$
6: −1

Day 2
1: $\frac{1}{343}$
2: $\frac{1}{26}$
3:
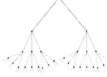
4: $\frac{1}{36}$
5: $\frac{1}{4}$
6: $\frac{1}{128}$

Day 3
1: $\frac{1}{52}$
2: 24
3: $\frac{1}{6}$
4: $\frac{1}{30}$
5: $\frac{1}{144}$
6: $\frac{1}{240}$

Day 4
1:

2: $\frac{1}{12}$
3: $\frac{1}{3}$
4: $\frac{1}{20}$
5: $\frac{1}{12}$
6: 35

Day 5
1: 1/60
2: 1/16
3: 1/9000
4: 1/343
5: $6s + 15t$

Day 6
$\frac{1}{72,000}$

WEEK 15

Day1
1: 5 inches
2: 32 ft
3: 36 ft
4: 27.56 mm
5: $\frac{1}{4}$
6: Distributive Property

Day 2
1: 16 cm
2: 16 feet
3: 6 feet
4: 4 inches
5: $11\frac{3}{20}$ inches
6: $\frac{-11}{4}$ or $-2\frac{3}{4}$

Day 3
1: 28.8 feet
2: 54 feet
3: 15 inches
4: 112.5 mm
5: 680 meters
6: 25.0

Day 4
1: 6 cm
2: 4.2 cm
3: 15 inches
4: 13.3 cm
5: 42 cm
6: $\frac{1}{216}$

Day 5
1: 18.75 feet
2: 11.73 inches
3: 28.125 feet
4: 5.8 cm
5: − $52.63

Day 6
31.25 cm X 20 cm

WEEK 16

Day 1
1: C
2: D
3: B
4: 14°
5: $17j\,(k + 3)$

Day 2
1: 30°
2: any length greater than 5.9 and less than 7.9 cm
3: 81.8°
4: 45°
5: divide by -4.2
6: 72 cm

Day 3
1: D
2: A
3: C
4: 71°
5: 18.5°

Day 4
1: 45°
2: 73.1°
3: any length greater than 9.2 inches but less than 12.5 inches
4: 66.5°
5: 184
6: $1163.51

Day 5
1: C
2: A
3: C
4: 111.7°
5: $\frac{8}{343}$

Day 6
57°

WEEK 17

Day 1
1: rectangle
2: circle
3: triangle
4: quadrilateral
5: oval
6: $\frac{2}{3}$

Day 2
1: trapezoid
2: circle
3: square
4: pentagon
5: rectangle
6: 7.5

Day 3
1: rectangle
2: circle
3: triangle
4: triangle
5: quadrilateral
6: 25.5 feet

Day 4
1: triangle
2: circle
3: oval
4: rectangle
5: circle
6: 27.5 feet

Day 5
1: circle
2: circle
3: quadrilateral
4: circle
5: square
6: $\frac{1}{16}$

Day 6
dodecagon

WEEK 18

Day1
1: 7 cm
2: 144π in^2
3: 10 cm
4: Circle A
5: Circle D

Day 2
1: 37.7 km
2: 30.25π in^2
3: Circle Z
4: Circle Y
5: Circle X
6: 60°

Day 3
1: 18.84 inches
2: 25π cm^2
3: 1 inch
4: 31.4 cm
5: 113.04 cm^2
6: rectangle

Day 4
1: Circle 4
2: Circle 1
3: 1, 3, 2, 4
4: 132.67 mm^2
5: 3 km
6: −4°F

Day 5
1: Circles 7 & 8
2: Circle 6
3: 7, 5, 6, 8
4: 144π meters^2
5: $15.12
6: 580

Day 6
16.25π yards^2

WEEK 19

Day 1
1: 65°
2: 59°
3: 31°
4: 126°
5: Compact & Economy

Day 2
1: 52°
2: 128°
3: 88°
4: circle
5: 35
6: 529

Day 3
1: 97°
2: 69°
3: 78°
4: 17.5°
5: 53°
6: 13c − 2

Day 4
1: vertical or opposite angles
2: supplementary
3: 37°
4: 143°
5: 15°
6: 61°

Day 5
1: 27°
2: 90°
3: supplementary
4: 53°
5: 127°
6: 19°

Day 6
Angle ACB is 60° and Angle BCD is 120°

WEEK 20

Day 1
1: 480 in^3
2: 392 in^2
3: 2,880 in^3
4: 47.5 feet^2
5: 47.5 feet^3
6: 71°

Day 2
1: 460 in^2
2: 11,040 in^3
3: 3,320 in^2
4: 180 in^2
5: 2,880 in^3
6: Commutative Property

Day 3
1: 17,280 in^3
2: 4,368 in^2
3: 114 ft^2
4: 105 ft^3
5: 924,000
6: 21°

Day 4
1: 4,995 cm^3
2: 1,816.5 cm^2
3: 797,475
4: 75°
5: 60°
6: 3.666...

Day 5
1: 141 in^2
2: 564 in^3
3: 402,187.5 cm^3
4: 9,250
5: $\frac{1}{8}$
6: 280

Day 6
It can be broken into:
6 triangles
2 trapezoids
1 rectangle + 2 triangles
OR 2 rectangles + 2 (or 4) triangles

End of Year Assessment

1: $\frac{7}{20}$

2: $\frac{13}{30}$

3: 35 in²

4: Commutative Property

5: 3

6: 64

7: 256π in²

8: 0.777...

9: 14 rows

10: likely

11: 68°

12: $6.32

13: $518.70

14: 180 in²

15: 65

16: 62°

17: $653.65

18: 18 cm x 31.5 cm

19: -1

20: 342 songs

21: $685.31

22: 80°

23: $655

24: $43 \frac{1}{3}$ km

25: 74 meters

26: square

27: B

28: D

29: C

30: A

31: D

32: D

33: A

34: C

35: C

36: D

37: B

38: B

39: D

40: C

41: A

42: D

43: C

Made in the USA
San Bernardino, CA
09 December 2017